INTERMEDIATE
ACCOUNTING 16E

Donald E. Kieso PhD, CPA
Northern Illinois University
DeKalb, Illinois

Jerry J. Weygandt PhD, CPA
University of Wisconsin—Madison
Madison, Wisconsin

Terry D. Warfield, PhD
University of Wisconsin—Madison
Madison, Wisconsin

WILEY

21 Accounting for Leases

LEARNING OBJECTIVES

After studying this chapter, you should be able to:

1 Understand the environment related to leasing transactions.

2 Explain the accounting for finance leases.

3 Explain the accounting for operating leases.

4 Discuss the accounting and reporting for special features of lease arrangements.

TIMES ARE A-CHANGING

Leasing has grown tremendously in popularity. Today, it is the fastest growing form of capital investment. Instead of borrowing money to buy an airplane, computer, nuclear core, or satellite, a company makes periodic payments to lease these assets. Even gambling casinos lease their slot machines. Of the 500 companies surveyed by the AICPA, more than half disclosed lease data.*

A classic example is the airline industry. Many travelers on airlines such as United, Delta, and Southwest believe these airlines own the planes on which they are flying. Often, this is not the case. Airlines lease many of their airplanes due to the favorable accounting treatment they received if they lease rather than purchase. Presented below are the lease percentages for the major U.S. airlines.

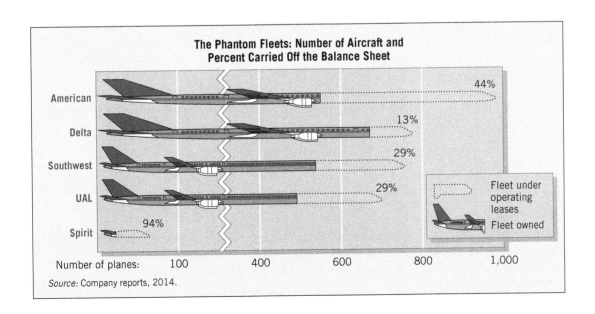

The Phantom Fleets: Number of Aircraft and Percent Carried Off the Balance Sheet

American 44%
Delta 13%
Southwest 29%
UAL 29%
Spirit 94%

Fleet under operating leases
Fleet owned

Number of planes: 100 400 600 800 1,000

Source: Company reports, 2014.

Accounting Trends and Techniques indicates that 277 out of 500 surveyed companies reported leased assets. Companies that lease tend to be smaller, are high growth, and are in technology-oriented industries (see *www.techlease.com*).

The same holds true for many other industries as well. What was this favorable accounting treatment? The previous FASB standard on leasing depended on whether a lease qualified as an operating lease or a finance lease. In an operating lease, companies did not report an asset on their balance sheet for the item they leased, nor did they report a related liability for their lease obligation. Only if the company had a finance lease would companies have to report an asset and a related liability on the balance sheet. However, the FASB has issued a new standard on leasing that mandates that all companies will have to report both assets and related liabilities for practically all lease arrangements.

This accounting change will have a significant impact on many companies' balance sheets. According to one study, companies listed on major stock exchanges are estimated to have over $3.3 trillion of leasing commitments, of which more than 85 percent do not appear on the listed companies' balance sheets. Companies with large off-balance-sheet operating leases will be most affected. For example, Walgreens recently had off-balance-sheet liabilities of $33,721 million, followed closely by AT&T with $31,047 million. Sir David Tweedie, the IASB's previous chairman, is known for saying that one day he would like to fly on an airplane that actually appears on that company's balance sheet. Well, Sir David, get ready because your wish is about to come true.

Sources: Adapted from Seth Lubore and Elizabeth MacDonald, "Debt? Who, Me?" *Forbes* (February 18, 2002), p. 56; A. Catanach and E. Ketz, "Still Searching for the 'Rite' Stuff," *Grumpy Old Accountants* (April 30, 2012), *http://blogs.smeal.psu.edu;* "Who Is Most Impacted by the New Lease Accounting Standards? An Analysis of the Fortune 500's Leasing Obligations," *Lease Accelerator* (2016); and Sue Lloyd, "A New Lease on Life," *Investor Perspective* (January 2016).

PREVIEW OF CHAPTER 21 Our opening story indicates the increased significance and prevalence of lease arrangements. As a result, the need for uniform accounting and informative reporting of these transactions has intensified. In this chapter, we look at the accounting issues related to leasing. The content and organization of this chapter are as follows.

This chapter also includes numerous conceptual and international discussions that are integral to the topics presented here.

ACCOUNTING FOR LEASES

THE LEASING ENVIRONMENT	FINANCE LEASES	OPERATING LEASES	SPECIAL LEASE ACCOUNTING PROBLEMS
• Lessees	• Lessee accounting	• Lessee accounting	• Residual values
• Lessee lease advantages	• Finance lease example	• Lessor accounting	• Other lease adjustments
• Lessors	• Lessor accounting		• Bargain purchase options
• Lessor lease advantages	• Sales-type lease example		• Short-term leases
• Conceptual nature of a lease			• Presentation, disclosure, and analysis
• Finance and operating leases			
• Lease classification			

REVIEW AND PRACTICE

Go to the REVIEW AND PRACTICE section at the end of the chapter for a targeted summary review and practice problem with solution. Multiple-choice questions with annotated solutions as well as additional exercises and practice problem with solutions are also available online.

LEARNING OBJECTIVE 1
Understand the environment related to leasing transactions.

THE LEASING ENVIRONMENT

A lease is a contractual agreement between a lessor and a lessee. This arrangement gives the lessee the right to use specific property, which is owned by the lessor, for a specified period of time. In return for the use of the property, the lessee makes rental payments over the lease term to the lessor.

A Look at the Lessee

Aristotle once said, "Wealth does not lie in ownership but in the use of things!" Clearly, many U.S. companies have decided that Aristotle is right, as they have become heavily involved in leasing assets rather than owning them. For example, according to the Equipment Leasing Association (ELA), the global equipment-leasing market is a $900 billion business, with the United States accounting for about one-third of the global market. The ELA estimates that of the $1.5 trillion in total fixed investment expected from domestic businesses in a recent year, $946 billion (63 percent) was financed through leasing. Remember that these statistics are just for equipment leasing. Add in real estate leasing, which is probably larger, and we are talking about a very large and growing business, one that was at least in part driven by the accounting.

What types of assets are being leased? As the opening story indicated, any type of equipment can be leased, such as railcars, helicopters, bulldozers, barges, CT scanners, computers, and so on. Illustration 21-1 summarizes what several major companies are leasing.

ILLUSTRATION 21-1
What Do Companies Lease?

Company (Ticker)	Description
Gap (GPS)	"We lease most of our store premises and some of our headquarters facilities and distribution centers."
ExxonMobil Corp. (XOM)	"Minimum commitments for operating leases, shown on an undiscounted basis, cover drilling equipment, tankers, service stations, and other properties."
JPMorgan Chase (JPM)	"JPMorgan Chase and its subsidiaries were obligated under a number of noncancelable operating leases for premises and equipment used primarily for banking purposes."
Maytag Corp. (MYG)	"The Company leases real estate, machinery, equipment, and automobiles under operating leases, some of which have renewal options."
McDonald's Corp. (MCD)	"The Company was the lessee at 15,235 restaurant locations through ground leases (the Company leases the land and the Company or franchisee owns the building) and through improved leases (the Company leases land and buildings)."
Starbucks Corp. (SBUX)	"Starbucks leases retail stores, roasting and distribution facilities, and office space under operating leases."
TXU Corp. (TXU)	"TXU Energy Holdings and TXU Electric Delivery have entered into operating leases covering various facilities and properties including generation plant facilities, combustion turbines, transportation equipment, mining equipment, data processing equipment, and office space."
Viacom Inc. (VIA.B)	"The Company has long-term non-cancelable operating lease commitments for office space and equipment, transponders, studio facilities, and vehicles. The Company also enters into leases for satellite transponders."

Source: Company 10-K filings.

The largest group of leased equipment involves information technology equipment, followed by assets in the transportation area (trucks, aircraft, rail), and then construction and agriculture.

Advantages of Leasing—Lessees

From the perspective of the lessee, leasing can provide significant advantages, such as the following:

1. *100% financing at fixed rates.* Leases are often signed without requiring any money down from the lessee. This helps the lessee conserve scarce cash—an especially desirable feature for new and developing companies. In addition, lease payments often remain fixed, which protects the lessee against inflation and increases in the cost of money. The following comment explains why companies choose a lease instead of a conventional loan: "Our local bank finally came up to 80 percent of the purchase price but wouldn't go any higher, and they wanted a floating interest rate. We just couldn't afford the down payment, and we needed to lock in a final payment rate we knew we could live with."

2. *Protection against obsolescence.* Leasing equipment reduces risk of obsolescence to the lessee and in many cases passes the risk of residual value to the lessor. For example, Merck (a pharmaceutical maker) leases computers. Under the lease agreement, Merck may turn in an old computer for a new model at any time, canceling the old lease and writing a new one. The lessor adds the cost of the new lease to the balance due on the old lease, less the old computer's trade-in value. As one treasurer remarked, "Our instinct is to purchase." But if a new computer is likely to come along in a short time, "then leasing is just a heck of a lot more convenient than purchasing." Naturally, the lessor also protects itself by requiring the lessee to pay higher rental payments or provide additional payments if the lessee does not maintain the asset.

3. *Flexibility.* Lease agreements may contain less restrictive provisions than other debt agreements. Innovative lessors can tailor a lease agreement to the lessee's special needs. For instance, the duration of the lease—the lease term—may be anything from a short period of time to the entire expected economic life of the asset. The rental payments may be level from year to year, or they may increase or decrease in amount. The payment amount may be predetermined or may vary with sales, the prime interest rate, the Consumer Price Index, or some other factor. In most cases, the rent is set to enable the lessor to recover the cost of the asset plus a fair return over the life of the lease.

4. *Less costly financing.* Some companies find leasing cheaper than other forms of financing. For example, start-up companies in depressed industries or companies in low tax brackets may lease to claim tax benefits that they might otherwise lose. Depreciation deductions offer no benefit to companies that have little if any taxable income. Through leasing, the leasing companies or financial institutions use these tax benefits. They can then pass some of these tax benefits back to the user of the asset in the form of lower rental payments.

A Look at the Lessor

Who are the lessors that own this property? They generally fall into one of three categories:

1. Banks.
2. Captive leasing companies.
3. Independents.

Banks

Banks are the largest players in the leasing business. They have low-cost funds, which give them the advantage of being able to purchase assets at less cost than their competitors. Banks have been aggressive in the leasing markets. Deciding that there is money to be made in leasing, banks have expanded their product lines in this area. Finally, leasing transactions are now quite standardized, which gives banks an advantage because they do not have to be as innovative in structuring lease arrangements. Thus, banks like Wells Fargo, Chase, Citigroup, and PNC have substantial leasing subsidiaries.

Captive Leasing Companies

Captive leasing companies are subsidiaries whose primary business is to perform leasing operations for the parent company. Companies like Caterpillar Financial Services Corp. (for Caterpillar), Ford Motor Credit (for Ford), and IBM Global Financing (for IBM) facilitate the sale of products to consumers. For example, suppose that Sterling Construction Co. wants to acquire a number of earthmovers from Caterpillar. In this case, Caterpillar Financial Services Corp. will offer to structure the transaction as a lease rather than as a purchase. Thus, Caterpillar Financial provides the financing rather than an outside financial institution.

Captive leasing companies have the point-of-sale advantage in finding leasing customers. That is, as soon as Caterpillar receives a possible equipment order, its leasing subsidiary can quickly develop a lease-financing arrangement. Furthermore, the captive lessor has product knowledge that gives it an advantage when financing the parent's product. The current trend is for captives to focus primarily on their companies' products rather than do general lease financing. For example, Boeing Capital and UPS Capital are two captives that have left the general finance business to focus exclusively on their parent companies' products.

Independents

Independents are the final category of lessors. Their market share has dropped fairly dramatically as banks and captive leasing companies have become more aggressive in the lease-financing area. Independents do not have point-of-sale access, nor do they have a low cost of funds advantage. What they are often good at is developing innovative contracts for lessees. In addition, they are starting to act as captive finance companies for some companies that do not have leasing subsidiaries. For example, International Lease Finance Corp. is one of the world's largest independent lessors. According to recent data from the *Equipment Leasing and Finance Foundation 2015 Annual Report* on new business volume by lessor type, banks hold about 55 percent of the market, followed by captives at 31 percent. Independents had the remaining 14 percent of new business.

Advantages of Leasing—Lessors

Lessors find leasing attractive because:

INTERNATIONAL PERSPECTIVE

Some companies "double dip" on the international level too. The leasing rules of the lessor's and lessee's countries may differ, permitting both parties to own the asset. Thus, both lessor and lessee receive the tax benefits related to depreciation.

1. It often provides **profitable interest margins**.
2. It can **stimulate sales** of a lessor's product whether it be from a dealer (lessor) or a manufacturer (lessor).
3. It often provides **tax benefits** to various parties in the lease, which enhances the return to all the parties involved, including the lessor. To illustrate, Boeing Aircraft might sell one of its 737 jet planes to a wealthy investor who does not need a plane but could use the tax benefit. The investor (the lessor) then leases the plane to a foreign airline, for which the tax benefit is of no use. Everyone gains. Boeing sells its airplane, the investor receives the tax benefit, and the foreign airline receives a lower rental rate because the lessor is able to use the tax benefit.
4. It can provide a **high residual value to the lessor** upon the return of the property at the end of the lease term. Residual values can sometimes provide large profits.

Citigroup at one time estimated that the commercial aircraft it was leasing to the airline industry would have a residual value of 5 percent of their purchase price. It turned out that they were worth 150 percent of their cost—a handsome profit. At the same time, if residual values decline, lessors can suffer losses when less-valuable leased assets are returned at the conclusion of the lease. At one time, automaker Ford took a $2.1 billion write-down on its lease portfolio, when rising gas prices spurred dramatic declines in the resale values of leased trucks and SUVs. Such residual value losses led Chrysler to get out of the leasing business altogether.

WHAT DO THE NUMBERS MEAN?   RESIDUAL VALUE REGRET

As you have learned, residual value profits are an important driver for the popularity of leasing for lessors, especially for leases of equipment and vehicles. However, the profitability of equipment leasing hinges on the lessors' ability to accurately estimate the residual value of the leased asset at the end of the lease so as to resell the asset at a profit when returned by the lessee. However, General Motors (GM) has learned that residual value profits are not guaranteed. Here is what happened.

GM took advantage of a government subsidy for electric vehicles of $7,500 to help drive down the cost of a lease for its electric car, the Chevy Volt. The taxpayer subsidies along with other GM incentives provided for low monthly lease payments, given the estimated residual value, and led to a full two-thirds of all Volt "sales" being attributed to leases. That's about three times the lease rate for the overall industry. The problems for GM started when the Volts came back at the end of the lease. Unfortunately for GM and other electric car enthusiasts, demand for electric cars without the incentives (which expired) has not been sustained, and resale values for Volts plummeted.

As a result, rather than reaping residual value profits, GM sustained losses for the Volt lease returns that sold for less than the original expected residual values. It's a double whammy for GM as the already low sales numbers for new Volts will be further hurt by the supply of low-priced Volts on the used car lot. Although it appears that GM made a bad bet on residual value profits on the Volt, there may be beneficiaries as those looking for a good deal on a Volt now have a supply of low-priced, used models to choose from.

Source: M. Modica, "Chevy Volt Resale Values Plunge as Lease Returns Hit Market," *http://nlpc.org/stories/2014/08/07/chevy-volt-resale-values-plunge-lease-returns-hit-market.*

Conceptual Nature of a Lease

A lease is defined as a "contract, or part of a contract, that conveys the right to control the use of identified property, plant or equipment (an identified asset) for a period of time in exchange for consideration." [1] A lease therefore conveys the use of an asset from one party (the lessor) to another (the lessee) without transferring ownership. Accounting for lease transactions is controversial, as the following example illustrates.

If Delta borrows $47 million on a 10-year note from Bank of America to purchase a Boeing 737 jet plane, Delta should report an asset and related liability at that amount on its balance sheet. Similarly if Delta purchases the 737 for $47 million directly from Boeing through an installment purchase over 10 years, it should report an asset and related liability (i.e., it should "capitalize" the installment transaction).

However, what if Delta **leases** the Boeing 737 for 10 years from International Lease Finance Corp. (ILFC)—the world's largest lessor of airplanes—through a non-cancelable lease transaction with payments of the same amount as the installment purchase transaction? In that case, opinion differs over how to report this transaction. The various views on capitalization of leases are as follows.

See the FASB Codification References (page 21-76).

1. *Do not capitalize any leased assets.* This view considers capitalization inappropriate because Delta does not own the property. Furthermore, a lease is an **"executory" contract** requiring continuing performance by both parties. Because companies do not currently capitalize other executory contracts (such as purchase commitments and employment contracts), they should not capitalize leases either.

2. *Capitalize leases that are similar to installment purchases.* This view holds that companies should report transactions in accordance with their economic substance.

Therefore, if companies capitalize installment purchases, they should also capitalize leases that have similar characteristics. For example, Delta makes the same payments over a 10-year period for either a lease or an installment purchase. Lessees make rental payments, whereas owners make mortgage payments.

3. *Capitalize all long-term leases*. This approach requires only the long-term right to use the property in order to capitalize. This property-rights approach capitalizes all long-term leases.

4. *Capitalize firm leases where the penalty for nonperformance is substantial*. A final approach advocates capitalizing only "firm" (non-cancelable) contractual rights and obligations. "Firm" means that it is unlikely to avoid performance under the lease without a severe penalty.

> **UNDERLYING CONCEPTS**
>
> The issue of how to report leases is the classic case of substance versus form. Although legal title does not technically pass in lease transactions, the benefits from the use of the property do transfer.

In short, the viewpoints range from no capitalization to capitalization of all long-term leases. The FASB has recently adopted the third approach, which requires companies to capitalize all long-term leases. The only exception to capitalization is that leases covering a term of less than one year do not have to be capitalized. The FASB indicates that the right to use property under the terms of the lease is an asset, and the lessee's commitment to make payments under the lease is a liability.[1] As a result, Delta records the right-of-use of the airplane as an asset on its balance sheet. It also records a liability for its obligation to make payments under the lease. The lessor of the aircraft (ILFC) records a receivable upon entering into the lease with Delta.

Finance and Operating Leases (Lessee)

As you will learn, companies classify lease arrangements as either finance or operating. In either case, **companies capitalize all leased assets and liabilities.** Therefore, the balance sheet for a company that uses either a finance lease or an operating lease will be the same. However, for income statement purposes, the reporting of financial information depends on whether the lease is classified as a finance lease or operating lease.

For a finance lease, the lessee recognizes interest expense on the lease liability over the life of the lease using the effective-interest method and records amortization expense on the right-of-use asset generally on a straight-line basis. A lessee therefore reports both interest expense and amortization of the right-of-use asset on the income statement. As a result, the total expense for the lease transaction is generally higher in the earlier years of the lease arrangement under a finance lease arrangement.

In an operating lease, the lessee also measures interest expense using the effective-interest method. However, the lessee amortizes the right-of-use asset such that the total lease expense is the same from period to period. In other words, for operating leases, only a single lease expense (comprised of interest on the liability and amortization of the right-of-use asset) is recognized on the income statement, typically on a straight-line basis. Illustrations of both these approaches are shown in the following sections.

Lease Classification

How do companies determine whether to use the finance method or the operating method? From the lessee's perspective, a lessee should classify a lease based on whether the arrangement is effectively a purchase of the underlying asset. If the lease transfers

---

[1] The FASB believes that the reporting of an asset and liability for a lease arrangement is consistent with its conceptual framework definition of assets and liabilities. That is, assets are probable future economic benefits obtained or controlled by a particular entity as a result of past transactions or events. Liabilities are probable future sacrifices of economic benefits arising from present obligations of a particular entity to transfer assets or provide services to other entities in the future as a result of past transactions or events. See "Elements of Financial Statements," *Statement of Financial Accounting Concepts No. 6* (Stamford, Conn.: FASB, December 1985), pp. ix and x.

control (or ownership) of the underlying asset to a lessee, then the lease is classified as a finance lease. In this situation, the lessee takes ownership or consumes the substantial portion of the underlying asset over the lease term. All leases that do not meet any of the finance lease tests are classified as operating leases. In an operating lease, a lessee **obtains the right to use the underlying asset** but not ownership of the asset itself.

For example, a lease may convey use of one floor of an office building for five years. At the end of the lease, the lessee vacates the floor and the lessor can then lease the floor to another tenant. So this lease (an operating lease) conveys right-of-use but not ownership; the lessee controls the leased asset only during the five-year lease. As we will see, the accounting for a lease classified as a finance lease (transfer of control or ownership) or an operating lease (transfer of right-of-use) reflects differences in control conveyed in a lease arrangement.

Illustration 21-2 presents the lease classification tests, which are used to determine whether a company should use the finance lease approach or the operating lease approach.

ILLUSTRATION 21-2
Lease Classification Tests

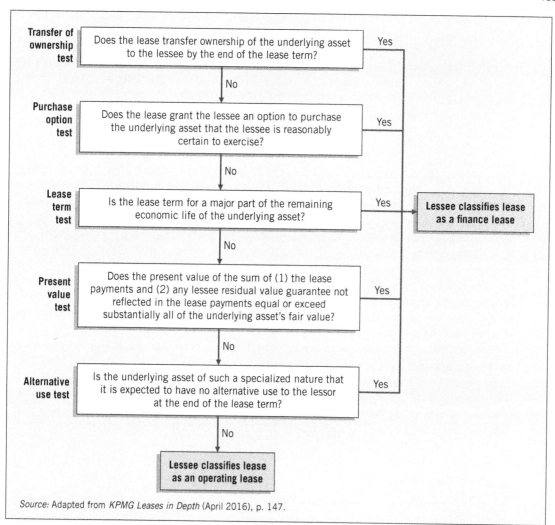

Source: Adapted from *KPMG Leases in Depth* (April 2016), p. 147.

For a lease to be a finance lease, it must be non-cancelable and **meet at least one of the five tests** listed in Illustration 21-2. **[2]** Otherwise, the lease is an operating lease. Additional explanation of each of the lease classification tests follows.

Transfer of Ownership Test

If the lease transfers ownership of the asset to the lessee, it is a finance lease. This test is not controversial and easily implemented in practice.

Purchase Option Test

A purchase option test is met if it is reasonably certain that the lessee will exercise the option. In other words, the lease purchase option allows the lessee to purchase the property for a price that is significantly lower than the underlying asset's expected fair value at the date the option becomes exercisable (hereafter referred to as a bargain purchase option).

For example, assume that Brett's Delivery Service leases a Honda Accord for $499 per month for 40 months, with an option to purchase the Accord for $100 at that end of the lease. If the estimated fair value of the Honda Accord is $3,000 at the end of the 40 months, the $100 option is clearly a bargain purchase option. Therefore, Brett's accounts for this lease as a finance lease.

Lease Term Test

When the lease term is a major part of the remaining economic life of the leased asset, companies should use the finance method in accounting for the lease transaction. The question is, what is a major part of the economic life of a leased asset? Although the FASB indicates that companies should use judgment in evaluating the lease term test, it recognizes that additional implementation guidance would be helpful. As a result, the Board establishes an implementation guideline that companies might use. That is, if the lease term is 75 percent or greater of the economic life of the leased asset, the lease meets the lease term test and finance lease treatment is appropriate (often referred to as the 75% test).[2] *This guideline should be used for homework purposes.*

Another factor to consider in the lease term test is a bargain renewal option. For example, a lease term is generally considered to be the fixed, non-cancelable term of the lease. However, a bargain renewal option allows the lessee to renew the lease for a rental that is lower than the expected fair rental at the time the option becomes exercisable. At the commencement of the lease, the difference between the renewal rental and the expected fair rental must be great enough to make exercise of the option to renew reasonably certain.[3] Thus, companies should include in the lease term any bargain renewal periods.

For example, assume that Home Depot leases Dell PCs for two years at a rental of $100 per month per computer. In addition, Home Depot can lease these computers for $10 per month per computer for another two years. The lease clearly offers a bargain renewal option, and Home Depot should consider the lease term for these computers to be four years, not two.

Present Value Test

If the present value of the lease payments is reasonably close to the fair value of the asset, a company is effectively purchasing the asset and should therefore use the finance method to account for the lease. Again, the FASB recognizes that determining what is reasonably close often involves significant judgment and therefore provides an implementation guideline (hereafter referred to as the 90% test). This guideline states that if the present value of the lease payments equals or exceeds 90 percent of the fair value of the asset, then a lessee should use the finance method to record the lease. *This guideline should be used for homework purposes.* To apply the present value test, a lessee must determine the amount of lease payments and the appropriate discount rate.

[2]Companies may lease a used asset in the last 25 percent of its economic life, which raises the question of applying the lease term test for classification of the lease. The FASB's position is that it is inconsistent to require that a lease covering the last few years be recorded as a finance lease by a lessee (or as a sales-type lease by a lessor) when a similar lease of that asset earlier in its economic life would have been classified as an operating lease. This conclusion is debatable because a lessee can direct the use of and obtain substantially all the remaining benefits from a significantly used asset just the same as it can a new or slightly used asset. **[3]**.

[3]Reasonably certain is a high threshold of probability. The FASB intended that parties to a lease account for options only when the lessee has a compelling economic reason to exercise a purchase, renewal, or termination option. **[4]**

Lease Payments. The lease payments generally include the following:

1. *Fixed payments.* These are the rental payments that are specified in the lease agreement and fixed over the lease term.

2. *Variable payments that are based on an index or a rate.* The lessee should include variable lease payments in the value of the lease liability at the level of the index/rate at the commencement date. When valuing the lease liability, no increases or decreases to future lease payments should be assumed based on increases or decreases in the index or rate. Instead, any difference in the payments due to changes in the index or rate is expensed in the period incurred. Illustrations 21-3 and 21-4 provide an analysis of variable lease payments.

INCLUDING VARIABLE LEASE PAYMENTS

Facts: On January 1, 2017, Jose Company leases an airplane for 6 years. The annual lease payments are $1,000,000 per year, payable at the beginning of each year (annuity-due basis). In addition, the lease agreement specifies that the lease payment increases by $30,000 every year.

Question: What are the lease payments in 2018?

Solution: On January 1, 2018, the lease payment is $1,030,000 ($1,000,000 + $30,000), which is considered a variable payment. Given that the amount of the variable payment is known from year to year (the rate is set at commencement of the lease and in substance fixed), such variable payments are included in calculating the present value of the lease liability.

ILLUSTRATION 21-3
Variable Lease Payments

EXPENSING VARIABLE LEASE PAYMENTS

Facts: Assume the same information as in Illustration 21-3, except that the lease payments are adjusted each year by a change in the Consumer Price Index (CPI).

Question: If the CPI is 100 at January 1, 2017, and increases to 104 on January 1, 2018, what is the payment on January 1, 2018?

Solution: The variable payment on January 1, 2018, is $1,040,000 ($1,000,000 × 1.04). Because the amount of the variable payment from year to year is not known at the lease commencement date, this payment is not included in determining the present value of the lease liability. This additional payment ($40,000) is recognized as an expense in the period it is incurred. Similarly, when lease payments vary with a performance measure (e.g., sales at a store location, asset usage), the variable amounts will be expensed in the period incurred.

ILLUSTRATION 21-4
Variable Lease Payments

3. *Amounts guaranteed by a lessee under a residual value guarantee.* Residual value is the expected value of the leased asset at the end of the lease term. A residual value can be guaranteed or unguaranteed. In a guaranteed residual value, the lessee has an obligation to not only return the leased asset at the end of the lease term but also to guarantee that the residual value will be a certain amount. If the lease involves an unguaranteed residual value, the lessee does not have any obligation to the lessor at the end of the lease, except to return the leased asset to the lessor. [5] For classification purposes, the lessee includes the full amount of the residual value guarantee at the end of the lease term in the present value test. The lessee does not consider unguaranteed residual value as part of the present value test.[4]

4. *Payments related to purchase or termination options that the lessee is reasonably certain to exercise.* As indicated earlier, if the lease contains a bargain purchase option, the cost of that option should be considered part of the lease payments. Analysis of a termination option is indicated in Illustration 21-5 (page 21-11).

---

[4]As discussed in more detail later, consideration of the guaranteed residual values differs for classification of the lease and measurement of the lease liability.

ILLUSTRATION 21-5
Termination Option

ANALYZING A TERMINATION OPTION

Facts: Cabrera Company leases a building and land from Worldwide Leasing for 6 years with monthly payments of $10,000. The lease contract allows Cabrera to terminate the lease after 2 years for a total payment of $140,000. At the commencement of the lease, it is reasonably certain that Cabrera will not continue the lease beyond 2 years.

Question: What are Cabrera's lease payments?

Solution: In this case, Cabrera should include the cost of the termination option in its calculation of the present value of its lease liability. The total lease payments are therefore $380,000 [($10,000 × 24) + $140,000].

Discount Rate. To determine whether the present value of the payments equals or exceeds 90 percent of the fair value of the leased asset, a lessee (like the Delta example presented earlier on page 21-6) should compute the present value of the lease payments using the implicit interest rate. **[6]** This rate is defined as the discount rate that, at commencement of the lease, causes the aggregate present value of the lease payments and unguaranteed residual value to be equal to the fair value of the leased asset. **[7]**

Delta (a lessee) may find that it is impracticable to determine the implicit rate of the lessor. In the event that it is impracticable to determine the implicit rate, Delta uses its incremental borrowing rate. The incremental borrowing rate is the rate of interest the lessee would have to pay on a similar lease or the rate that, at commencement of the lease, the lessee would incur to borrow over a similar term the funds necessary to purchase the asset. The implicit rate of the lessor is generally a more realistic rate to use in determining the amount to report as the asset and related liability for Delta. However, given the difficulty the lessee may have in determining the implicit rate, it is likely that the lessee will use the incremental borrowing rate.[5]

Alternative Use Test

If at the end of the lease term the lessor does not have an alternative use for the asset, the lessee classifies the lease as a finance lease. In this situation, the assumption is that the lessee uses all the benefits from the leased asset and therefore the lessee has essentially purchased the asset.

Lessors sometimes build an asset to meet specifications set by the lessee (referred to as "build-to-suit" arrangements). For example, an equipment manufacturer might build hydraulic lifts to meet unique loading dock configurations of a lessee, like Amazon.com. Given the specialty nature of the equipment, only Amazon can use the lifts and it receives substantially all of the benefits of the leased asset, such that the alternative use test is met.

LEARNING OBJECTIVE 2
Explain the accounting for finance leases.

ACCOUNTING FOR FINANCE LEASES

As indicated, the accounting for a lease arrangement by lessees and lessors depends on classification of the lease as a sale of the underlying asset. If the lease is in substance a sale, the lease is classified as a finance lease.

Lessee Accounting for Finance Leases

To illustrate the accounting for a finance lease, assume that Caterpillar Financial Services Corp. (a subsidiary of **Caterpillar**) and Sterling Construction sign a lease agreement dated January 1, 2017, that calls for Caterpillar to lease a backhoe to Sterling beginning January 1, 2017. The terms and provisions of the lease agreement and other pertinent data are as follows.

[5]This difficulty arises because, for example, the lessee may not know the residual value used by the lessor, nor the initial direct costs that the lessor incurs.

- The term of the lease is five years. The lease agreement is non-cancelable, requiring equal rental payments of $20,711.11 at the beginning of each year (annuity-due basis).

- The backhoe has a fair value at the commencement of the lease of $100,000, an estimated economic life of five years, and a guaranteed residual value of $5,000. (Sterling expects that it is probable that the expected value of the residual value at the end of the lease will be greater than the guaranteed amount of $5,000.)

- The lease contains no renewal options. The backhoe reverts to Caterpillar at the termination of the lease.

- Sterling's incremental borrowing rate is 5 percent per year.

- Sterling depreciates, on a straight-line basis, similar equipment that it owns.

- Caterpillar sets the annual rental rate to earn a rate of return of 4 percent per year; Sterling is aware of this rate.

Sterling evaluates the lease classification tests as indicated in Illustration 21-6.

ILLUSTRATION 21-6
Lease Classification Tests

Test	Assessment
1. Transfer of ownership test	Transfer of ownership does not occur; the asset reverts to Caterpillar at the end of the lease.
2. Purchase option test	There is no purchase option in the lease.
3. Lease term test	The lease term is equal to the economic life of the asset (100 percent). Therefore, **the lease meets the lease term test**.
4. Present value test	The present value of the lease payments is $100,000*, which is 100 percent (greater than or equal to 90 percent) of the fair value of the backhoe. Therefore, **the lease meets the present value test.**
5. Alternative use test	Since the asset is returned to Caterpillar with some residual value, the alternative use test is not met.

Present value of payments ($20,711.11 × 4.62990 (*PVF-AD$_{5,4\%}$))	$ 95,890.35[6]
Present value of the residual value ($5,000 × .82193 (*PVF$_{5,4\%}$*))	4,109.65
	$100,000.00

Thus, the lease is classified as a finance lease due to meeting the lease term, present value, and alternative use tests (meeting any one of these tests would suffice). Note that the present value test includes the full amount of the residual value guarantee to determine whether the lease is classified as a financing or operating lease. However, for measurement of the lease liability, Sterling includes **only the expected residual value probable of being owed by the lessee under the residual value guarantee. [8]** Because Sterling believes that it is probable that the expected residual value will be greater than the guaranteed residual value, the guaranteed residual value is not included in the measurement of the lease liability.[7]

Sterling computes the lease liability and the amount capitalized as a right-of-use asset as the present value of the lease payments, as shown in Illustration 21-7.

ILLUSTRATION 21-7
Present Value of Lease Payments

Capitalized amount = $20,711.11 × Present value of an annuity due of 1 for 5 periods at 4%	
= $20,711.11 × 4.62990 (*PVF-OA$_{5,4\%}$*)	
= $95,890.35*	
*Rounded by $0.02.	

[6]The computation of the present value is rounded by $0.02. The rounding occurs because the tables from Chapter 6 (pages 314–323) are used to determine the amounts shown. *For homework and other computations in the text, we use the tables which may lead to small rounding differences.* In practice, a financial calculator is often used to avoid these rounding differences.

[7]Later in the chapter, we provide an expanded discussion of the relationship between the expected residual value and the guaranteed residual value, and its effect on the measurement of the lease liability.

Sterling uses Caterpillar's implicit interest rate of 4 percent instead of its incremental borrowing rate of 5 percent because the implicit rate is known to Sterling.[8] Sterling records the lease on its books as follows.

January 1, 2017

Right-of-Use Asset	95,890.35	
Lease Liability		95,890.35

Note that Sterling records the obligation at the net amount of $95,890.35 (the present value of the lease payments) rather than at the gross amount of $103,555.55 ($20,711.11 × 5).[9] Sterling then records the **first lease payment** as follows.

January 1, 2017

Lease Liability	20,711.11	
Cash		20,711.11

The annual interest expense, applying the effective-interest method, is a function of the outstanding liability as shown in the lease amortization schedule in Illustration 21-8.

ILLUSTRATION 21-8
Lease Amortization
Schedule

STERLING CONSTRUCTION
LEASE AMORTIZATION SCHEDULE
ANNUITY-DUE BASIS

Date	Annual Lease Payment	Interest (4%) on Liability	Reduction of Lease Liability	Lease Liability
	(a)	(b)	(c)	(d)
1/1/17				$95,890.35
1/1/17	$ 20,711.11	$ –0–	$20,711.11	75,179.24
1/1/18	20,711.11	3,007.17	17,703.94	57,475.30
1/1/19	20,711.11	2,299.01	18,412.10	39,063.20
1/1/20	20,711.11	1,562.53	19,148.58	19,914.62
1/1/21	20,711.11	796.49*	19,914.62	0.00
	$103,555.55	$7,665.20	$95,890.35	

(a) Lease payment as required by lease.
(b) Four percent of the preceding balance of (d) except for 1/1/17; since this is an annuity due, no time has elapsed at the date of the first payment and therefore no interest has accrued.
(c) (a) minus (b).
(d) Preceding balance minus (c).

*Rounded by $0.09.

Each lease payment of $20,711.11 consists of two elements: (1) a reduction of the lease liability and (2) a financing cost (interest expense).[10] The total financing cost (interest expense) over the term of the lease is $7,665.20. This amount is the difference between the present value of the lease payments ($95,890.35) and the actual cash disbursed ($103,555.55). Sterling records **interest expense** for the first year of the lease as follows.

December 31, 2017

Interest Expense	3,007.17	
Lease Liability		3,007.17

[8]If Sterling had not known Caterpillar's implicit rate, it would have used its incremental borrowing rate of 5 percent to compute the present value of the lease liability.

[9]As discussed, in measuring the liability and right-of-use asset, Sterling does not include the present value of the residual value because the guaranteed amount is not greater than the expected amount. We discuss residual value considerations in more detail in a later section of the chapter.

[10]Because it occurs at the lease commencement date, the first payment does not contain an interest component.

Amortization of the right-of-use asset over the five-year lease term, applying Sterling's normal depreciation policy (straight-line method), results in the following entry at December 31, 2017.

December 31, 2017

Amortization Expense	19,178.07	
Right-of-Use Asset ($95,890.35 ÷ 5 years)		19,178.07

At December 31, 2017, Sterling reports right-of-use assets and related lease liabilities separately from other assets and liabilities on its balance sheet, or discloses these assets and liabilities in the notes to its financial statements.

Sterling classifies the portion of the liability due within one year or the operating cycle, whichever is longer, with current liabilities, and the rest with noncurrent liabilities. For example, the current portion of the December 31, 2017, total obligation of $75,179.24 in Sterling's amortization schedule is the amount payable in 2018, or $20,711.11. Note that this current portion is composed of two components: (1) accrued interest on the liability outstanding throughout the year ($3,007.17) and (2) reduction of the initial lease liability ($17,703.94). Illustration 21-9 shows the presentation of the lease assets and liabilities sections as they relate to lease transactions at December 31, 2017, assuming Sterling chose to present right-of-use assets and lease liabilities separately from other assets and liabilities on the balance sheet.

Noncurrent assets	
Right-of-use assets ($95,890.35 − $19,178.07)	$76,712.28
Current liabilities	
Lease liability ($3,007.17 + $17,703.94)	$20,711.11
Noncurrent liabilities	
Lease liability	57,475.30

ILLUSTRATION 21-9
Balance Sheet Presentation

On its December 31, 2017, income statement, Sterling reports interest expense on the liability and amortization expense related to right-of-use assets, as shown in Illustration 21-10.

Expenses	
Interest expense (lease liabilities)	$ 3,007.17
Amortization expense (right-of-use assets)	19,178.07

ILLUSTRATION 21-10
Income Statement Presentation

Sterling records the second lease payment as follows.

January 1, 2018

Lease Liability ($3,007.17 + $17,703.95)	20,711.11	
Cash		20,711.11

Entries through 2021 follow the pattern above. **Upon expiration of the lease,** Sterling has fully amortized the amount capitalized as a right-of-use asset. It also has fully discharged its lease obligation. At the date the lease expires, both the right-of-use asset account and lease liability account related to Sterling's lease of the backhoe have zero balances. If Sterling does not purchase the backhoe, it returns the equipment to Caterpillar.[11]

---

[11]If Sterling purchases the backhoe during the term of the lease, it accounts for the transaction as a termination of the lease and a purchase of an asset. Thus, it would record any difference between the purchase price and the carrying amount of the lease liability as an adjustment of the carrying amount of the asset. [9]

If Sterling purchases the equipment from Caterpillar at the termination of the lease at a price of $5,000 and the estimated remaining life of the equipment is two years, it makes the following entry.

January 1, 2022

Equipment	5,000	
Cash		5,000

Lessor Accounting for Sales-Type Leases

We now turn our attention to the other party involved in the Caterpillar/Sterling lease arrangement—Caterpillar (the lessor). The **lease classification tests for the lessor are identical to the tests used by the lessee** to determine classification of a lease as a financing or operating lease, as shown in Illustration 21-6 (on page 21-12). Why use the same criteria for both the lessee and the lessor? The reason is that the tests are used to determine whether the lessee and the lessor have an agreement to transfer control of the asset from one party to the other. If the lessee receives control, then the lessor must have given up control.

The FASB concluded that by meeting any of the lease classification tests in Illustration 21-6, the lessor transfers control of the leased asset and therefore satisfies a performance obligation, which is required for revenue recognition under the FASB's recent standard on revenue. **[10]** That is, the lessor has, in substance, transferred control of the right-of-use asset and therefore has a sales-type lease if the lessee takes ownership or consumes a substantial portion of the underlying asset over the lease term. On the other hand, if the lease does not transfer control of the asset over the lease term, the lessor will generally use the operating approach in accounting for the lease. **[11]** Although not part of the classification tests, the lessor must also determine whether the collectibility of payments from the lessee is probable. If payments are not probable, the lessor does not record a receivable and does not derecognize the leased asset. Instead, receipt of any lease payments is recorded as a deposit liability. **[12]**[12]

WHAT DO THE NUMBERS MEAN?   NOT SO FAST

As an illustration of the importance of the control criteria, consider the case of computer leasing companies, which at one time bought IBM equipment, leased the equipment to their customers, and removed the leased assets from their balance sheets. In leasing the assets, the computer lessors stated that they would substitute new IBM equipment if obsolescence occurred (a sales return provision). However, when IBM introduced a new computer line, IBM refused to sell it to the computer leasing companies. As a result, a number of the lessors could not meet their contracts with their customers and had to take back the old equipment. Thus, control had not been fully transferred and the computer leasing companies therefore had to reinstate the assets they had taken off the books. Such a case demonstrates one reason why the lessor classification tests must be aligned with those for revenue recognition.

Accounting Measurement and Presentation

Classification of the lease as either a sales-type or operating lease determines the subsequent accounting by the lessor.[13] For a sales-type lease, the lessor accounts for the lease in a manner similar to the sale of an asset. Under a sales-type lease, the lessor generally records a Lease Receivable and eliminates the leased asset. The lease receivable for Sterling is computed as shown in Illustration 21-11.[14]

---

[12]If classified as an operating lease and collectibility is not probable, recognition of lease income is limited to cash received.

[13]We call it a sales-type lease because there is another type of lease for a lessor that uses the finance method, called a "direct financing lease." Direct financing leases are not that common in practice; we discuss this exception in Appendix 21B.

[14]Lease Receivable is often defined as only the present value of the rental payments plus the present value of the guaranteed residual value. In the case in which the lessor has an unguaranteed residual value, the total amount is often referred to as the **net investment** in the lease. Another approach is to report the unguaranteed residual value separately when making the journal entry. *We use the definition in Illustration 21-11 for pedagogical reasons; this definition (including both guaranteed and unguaranteed residual values) should be used in the homework.*

ILLUSTRATION 21-11
Lease Receivable

Lease Receivable	=	Present Value of Rental Payments	+	Present Value of Guaranteed and Unguaranteed Residual Values

Any selling profit on the transfer of the leased asset is recognized by recording sales revenue and related cost of goods sold at the commencement of the lease. The lessor recognizes interest revenue on the lease receivable over the life of the lease using the effective-interest method.[15]

Sales-Type Lease Example

To illustrate lessor accounting for a sales-type lease, refer to the preceding Caterpillar/ Sterling example (on pages 21-11 to 21-15). We repeat here the information relevant to Caterpillar in accounting for this lease transaction.

- The term of the lease is five years. The lease agreement is non-cancelable, requiring equal rental payments at the beginning of each year (annuity-due basis).

- The backhoe has a fair value at the commencement of the lease of $100,000, an estimated economic life of five years, and a guaranteed residual value of $5,000 (which is less than the expected residual value of the backhoe at the end of the lease). Further, assume the underlying asset (the backhoe) has an $85,000 cost to the dealer, Caterpillar.

- The lease contains no renewal options. The backhoe reverts to Caterpillar at the termination of the lease.

- Collectibility of payments by Caterpillar is probable.

- Caterpillar sets the annual rental payment to earn a rate of return of 4 percent per year (implicit rate) on its investment as shown in Illustration 21-12.

ILLUSTRATION 21-12
Lease Payment Calculation

Fair value of leased equipment	$100,000.00
Less: Present value of the residual value ($5,000 × .82193 $(PVF_{5,4\%})$)	4,109.65
Amount to be recovered by lessor through lease payments	$ 95,890.35
Five beginning-of-year lease payments to earn a 4% return ($95,890.35 ÷ 4.62990 $(PVF\text{-}AD_{5,4\%})$)	$ 20,711.11

Caterpillar determines the lease payments based on the implicit rate (rate of return) needed to justify leasing the asset. In establishing this rate of return, Caterpillar considers the credit standing of Sterling, the term of the lease, and whether the residual value is guaranteed or unguaranteed. In the Caterpillar/Sterling example, when a residual value is involved (whether guaranteed or not), Caterpillar does not have to recover as much from the rental payments and therefore the rental payments are less.

The lease meets the criteria for classification as a finance (sales-type) lease because (1) the present value of the lease payments is equal to the fair value of the asset, and (2) the lease term is equal to the economic life of the asset. That is, Sterling will consume substantially the entire underlying asset over the lease term. Caterpillar computes the lease receivable as shown in Illustration 21-13.

---

[15]Even if the selling profit is zero (or a net loss), the lessor recognizes sales and cost of goods sold. For a lease classified as operating, the lessor continues to recognize the asset on its books and records lease revenue for payments received from the lease over the lease term.

ILLUSTRATION 21-13
Lease Receivable
Calculation

Lease receivable = Present value of the rental payment + Present value of the guaranteed
residual value
= $95,890.35 ($20,711.12 × 4.62990 (PVF-OA$_{5,4\%}$)) + $4,109.65 ($5,000.00 ×
.82193 (PVF$_{5,4\%}$))
= $100,000.00

Caterpillar then records the lease receivable, cost of goods sold, and sales revenue and removes the leased asset (which prior to the lease was included in Caterpillar's inventory). The journal entry to record this transaction on January 1, 2017, is as follows.

January 1, 2017

Lease Receivable	100,000	
Cost of Goods Sold	85,000	
Sales Revenue		100,000
Inventory		85,000

As a result, Caterpillar reports a gross profit of $15,000 ($100,000 – $85,000) on its income statement. Caterpillar then prepares a lease amortization schedule, as shown in Illustration 21-14, applying the effective-interest method and recognizing interest revenue as a function of the lease receivable balance.

ILLUSTRATION 21-14
Lease Amortization
Schedule

CATERPILLAR FINANCIAL
LEASE AMORTIZATION SCHEDULE
ANNUITY-DUE BASIS

Date	Annual Lease Payment	Interest (4%) on Lease Receivable	Reduction of Lease Receivable	Lease Receivable
	(a)	(b)	(c)	(d)
1/1/17				$100,000.00
1/1/17	$ 20,711.11	$ –0–	$ 20,711.11	79,288.89
1/1/18	20,711.11	3,171.56	17,539.55	61,749.34
1/1/19	20,711.11	2,469.97	18,241.14	43,508.20
1/1/20	20,711.11	1,740.33	18,970.78	24,537.42
1/1/21	20,711.11	981.50	19,729.61	4,807.81
1/1/22	5,000.00	192.19*	4,807.81	0.00
	$108,555.55	$8,555.55	$100,000.00	

(a) Lease payment as required by lease.
(b) Four percent of the preceding balance of (d) except for 1/1/17; since this is an annuity due, no time has elapsed at the date of the first payment and therefore no interest has accrued.
(c) (a) minus (b).
(d) Preceding balance minus (c).

*Rounded by $0.12.

On January 1, 2017, Caterpillar records receipt of the first year's lease payment as follows.

January 1, 2017

Cash	20,711.11	
Lease Receivable		20,711.11

On December 31, 2017, Caterpillar recognizes the interest revenue on the lease receivable during the first year through the following entry.

December 31, 2017

Lease Receivable	3,171.56	
Interest Revenue		3,171.56

UNDERLYING CONCEPTS

Interest revenue for the lessor may differ from interest expense for the lessee because the lease receivable amount is different than that for the lease liability.

At December 31, 2017, Caterpillar reports the lease receivable in its balance sheet among current assets and noncurrent assets. It classifies the portion due within one year or the operating cycle, whichever is longer, as a current asset, and the rest with noncurrent assets.

Illustration 21-15 shows Caterpillar's assets section as it relates to the Sterling lease transactions at December 31, 2017.

ILLUSTRATION 21-15
Balance Sheet Presentation

Current assets	
Lease receivable ($3,171.56 + $17,539.56)	$20,711.11
Noncurrent assets (investments)	
Lease receivable	61,749.34

In its income statement for 2017, Caterpillar presents the revenue and expense items shown in Illustration 21-16.

ILLUSTRATION 21-16
Income Statement
Presentation

Sales	
Sales revenue	$100,000.00
Less: Cost of goods sold	85,000.00
Other revenue	
Interest revenue	3,171.56

The following entries record receipt of the second year's lease payment and recognition of the interest revenue in 2018.

January 1, 2018

Cash	20,711.11	
Lease Receivable		20,711.11

December 31, 2018

Lease Receivable	2,469.97	
Interest Revenue		2,469.97

Journal entries through 2021 follow the same pattern, except for the year 2021. In 2021, the final lease payment is made on January 1, 2021, but the asset is not returned to Caterpillar until January 1, 2022.

Caterpillar makes the following entry on December 31, 2021.

December 31, 2021

Lease Receivable	192.19	
Lease Revenue		192.19

As a result, interest revenue of $192.19 is recognized for the year 2021 as the residual value accretes up to $5,000 at the end of the lease. At January 1, 2022, when the leased asset is returned to Caterpillar, the Lease Receivable account is reduced to zero and the asset returned is recorded in inventory, as follows.

January 1, 2022

Inventory	5,000	
Lease Receivable		5,000

ACCOUNTING FOR OPERATING LEASES

Lessee Accounting for Operating Leases

If a lease does not meet any of the lease classification tests for a finance lease, a lessee should classify it as an operating lease. For leases classified as operating, the lessee records a right-of-use asset and lease liability at commencement of the lease, similar to the finance lease approach. However, unlike a finance lease, the lessee records the same amount for lease expense each period over the lease term (often referred to as the straight-line method for expense measurement).

Companies continue to use the effective-interest method for amortizing the lease liability. However, instead of reporting interest expense, a lessee reports interest on the lease liability as part of Lease Expense. In addition, the lessee no longer reports amortization expense related to the right-of-use asset. Instead, it "plugs" in an amount that increases the Lease Expense account so that it is the same amount from period to period. This plugged amount then reduces the right-of-use asset, such that both the right-of-use asset and the lease liability are amortized to zero at the end of the lease.[16]

To illustrate operating lease accounting for a lessee, assume that Josway Disposal Inc. (lessor) and Traylor Stores Inc. (lessee) sign a lease agreement dated January 1, 2017. The lease agreement specifies that Josway will grant right-of-use of one of its standard cardboard compactors (is not of a specialized nature) at one of Traylor's locations. Information relevant to the lease is as follows.

- The lease agreement is non-cancelable with a term of three years.

- The compactor has a cost and fair value at commencement of the lease of $60,000, an estimated economic life of five years, and a residual value at **the end of the lease** of $12,000 (unguaranteed).

- The lease contains no renewal options. The lift reverts to Josway at the termination of the lease.

- The implicit rate of Josway (the lessor) is 6 percent and is known by Traylor.

Josway determines the rental payments such that it earns rate of return of 6 percent per year on its investment, as shown in Illustration 21-17.

ILLUSTRATION 21-17
Computation of Lease Payments

Fair value of leased equipment	$60,000.00
Less: Present value of the residual value ($12,000 × .83962 (PVF$_{3,6\%}$))	10,075.44
Amount to be recovered by lessor through lease payments	$49,924.56
Three beginning-of-year lease payments to earn a 6% return ($49,924.56 ÷ 2.83339 (PVF-AD$_{3,6\%}$))	$17,620.08

Traylor classifies the lease as an operating lease because none of the finance lease tests are met, as shown in Illustration 21-18.

ILLUSTRATION 21-18
Lease Classification Tests

Test	Assessment
1. Transfer of ownership test	Transfer of ownership does not occur; the asset reverts to Josway at the end of the lease.
2. Purchase option test	There is no purchase option in the lease.
3. Lease term test	The lease term is 60 percent (3 ÷ 5) of the economic life of the asset, which is less than a major part of the life of the asset (75 percent).
4. Present value test	The present value of the lease payments is $49,924.56*, which is 83.2% ($49,924.56 ÷ $60,000) of the fair value of the compactor. Therefore, the lease does not meet the present value test.
5. Alternative use test	As indicated, the equipment is not of a specialized nature and is expected to have use to Josway when returned at the end of the lease.

*$17,620.08 × 2.83339 (PVF-AD$_{3,6\%}$)

Traylor makes the following entry to record this operating lease.

January 1, 2017

Right-of-Use Asset	49,924.56	
Lease Liability		49,924.56

[16]The FASB indicates that reporting a single operating cost in the income statement more appropriately reflects the economics of an operating lease than the separate recognition of interest and amortization used in a finance lease. The rationale for this approach is that an operating lease grants different rights to the lessee. The different rights are that in an operating lease, the lessee is not exposed to nor benefits from any value changes in the right-of-use asset over the term of the lease. **[13]**

In addition, Traylor records the first payment, as follows.

January 1, 2017

Lease Liability	17,620.08	
Cash		17,620.08

Traylor then prepares a lease amortization schedule, as shown in Illustration 21-19, applying the effective-interest method and measuring interest on the liability as a function of the lease liability balance, with related amortization of the lease liability.

ILLUSTRATION 21-19
Lease Amortization
Schedule

TRAYLOR STORES INC.
LEASE AMORTIZATION SCHEDULE
ANNUITY-DUE BASIS

Date	Annual Lease Payment (a)	Interest (6%) on Liability (b)	Reduction of Lease Liability (c)	Lease Liability (d)
1/1/17				$49,924.56
1/1/17	$17,620.08	$ –0–	$17,620.08	32,304.48
1/1/18	17,620.08	1,938.27	15,681.81	16,622.67
1/1/19	17,620.08	997.41*	16,622.67	0.00
	$52,860.24	$2,935.68	$49,924.56	

(a) Lease payment as required by lease.
(b) Six percent of the preceding balance of (d) except for 1/1/17; since this is an annuity due, no time has elapsed at the date of the first payment and therefore no interest has accrued.
(c) (a) minus (b).
(d) Preceding balance minus (c).

*Rounded by $0.05.

To record equal amounts of lease expense each period under the straight-line approach, the lessee computes interest on the lease liability (as shown in Illustration 21-19) and then amortizes the right-of-use asset in a manner that results in equal amounts of lease expense in each period. Traylor computes the straight-line lease expense each year as presented in the lease expense schedule in Illustration 21-20.

ILLUSTRATION 21-20
Lease Expense Schedule

TRAYLOR STORES INC.
LEASE EXPENSE SCHEDULE

Date	(A) Lease Expense (Straight-Line)	(B) Interest (6%) on Liability	(C) Amortization of ROU Asset (A − B)	(D) Carrying Value of ROU Asset (D − C)
1/1/17				$49,924.56
12/31/17	$17,620.08	$1,938.27	$15,681.81	34,242.75
12/31/18	17,620.08	997.41	16,622.67	17,620.08
12/31/19	17,620.08		17,620.08	0.00
	$52,860.24	$2,935.68	$49,924.56	

As shown in Illustration 21-20, Traylor does the following to record straight-line expense related to its operating lease.

1. Traylor makes lease payments totaling $52,860.24 to Josway. Traylor divides the $52,860.24 by the lease term of three years to compute its straight-line annual lease expense of $17,620.08 (Column A).

2. Traylor records part of its annual lease expense based on interest related to amortizing its lease liability according to the lease amortization schedule provided in Illustration 21-19 [Column (b)].

3. Traylor deducts that amount of interest on the liability from the straight-line lease expense to arrive at the amount of amortization of the right-of-use asset (Column C).

4. Traylor determines the carrying value of the right-of-use asset by deducting the amortization of the right-of-use asset each reporting period (Column D).

Traylor prepares journal entries during the lease term to record lease expense, which is comprised of interest on the lease liability and the amortization of the right-of-use asset. Traylor makes the following entry to record lease expense in 2017 on December 31, 2017.

December 31, 2017

Lease Expense	17,620.08	
Right-of-Use Asset ($17,620.08 − $1,938.27)		15,681.81
Lease Liability		1,938.27

As indicated in Illustration 21-20, Traylor accrues interest ($1,938.27) and amortizes the right-of-use asset ($15,681.81). As a result, Traylor records a single lease expense amount of $17,620.08 for the year 2017. The second lease payment on January 1, 2018, is as follows.

January 1, 2018

Lease Liability ($1,938.27 + $15,681.81)	17,620.08	
Cash		17,620.08

Journal entries in subsequent periods follow the same pattern, using the amounts presented in Illustration 21-19. The entry to record lease expense in the second year of the lease is as follows.

December 31, 2018

Lease Expense	17,620.08	
Right-of-Use Asset ($17,620.08 − $997.41)		16,622.67
Lease Liability		997.41

Traylor records a single lease expense amount of $17,620.08, comprised of interest on the lease liability ($997.41 in 2018) and amortization of the right-of-use asset ($16,622.67 in 2018). The third and final lease payment is made on January 1, 2019, as follows.

January 1, 2019

Lease Liability ($997.41 + $16,622.47)	17,620.08	
Cash		17,620.08

Traylor makes the following entry to record lease expense for 2019, the third year of the lease.

December 31, 2019

Lease Expense	17,620.08	
Right-of-Use Asset		17,620.08

Following this entry, the right-of-use asset has been fully amortized. As summarized in the lease expense schedule in Illustration 21-20, the total lease expense for the three years is comprised of the amortization of the right-of-use asset of $49,924.56 plus interest related to the lease liability of $2,935.68, for a total lease expense of $52,860.24. Traylor presents the interest and right-of-use asset amortization related to the lease as a **single lease expense** in the income statement each year.

Lessor Accounting for Operating Leases

To illustrate lessor accounting for an operating lease, refer to the previously discussed lease agreement between Josway Disposal Inc. and Traylor Stores Inc. for the use of one of Josway's standard cardboard compactors. Information relevant to the lease is as follows.

- The term of the lease is three years. The lease agreement is non-cancelable, requiring three annual rental payments of $17,620.08, with the first payment on January 1, 2017 (annuity-due basis).

- The compactor has a cost and fair value at commencement of the lease of $60,000, an estimated economic life of five years, and a residual value at the end of the lease of $12,000 (unguaranteed).

- The lease contains no renewal options. The compactor reverts to Josway at the termination of the lease.

- The implicit rate of the lessor is known by Traylor. Traylor's incremental borrowing rate is 6 percent. Josway sets the annual rental rate to earn a rate of return of 6 percent per year (implicit rate) on its investment, as shown in Illustration 21-17 (page 21-19).

Applying the same classification tests used by Traylor (see Illustration 21-18 on page 21-19), Josway classifies the lease as an operating lease because none of the finance lease tests are met. Under the operating method, Josway (the lessor) continues to recognize the asset on its balance sheet and recognizes lease revenue (generally on a straight-line basis) in each period. Josway **depreciates the leased asset using double-declining-balance**.

To illustrate the operating method for the Josway/Traylor lease, Josway records the lease payment on a straight-line basis on January 1, 2017, 2018, and 2019, as follows.

January 1, 2017, 2018, and 2019

Cash	17,620.08	
Unearned Lease Revenue		17,620.08

On December 31, 2017, 2018, and 2019, Josway records the recognition of the revenue each period as follows.

Unearned Lease Revenue	17,620.08	
Lease Revenue		17,620.08

Josway also records depreciation expense on the leased equipment (assuming double-declining-balance, given a cost basis of $60,000, and a five-year economic life), as follows.

Depreciation Expense ($60,000 × 40%)	24,000.00	
Accumulated Depreciation—Equipment		24,000.00

In addition to depreciation expense, Josway records other costs related to the lease arrangement, such as insurance, maintenance, and taxes in the period incurred. Josway classifies the leased equipment and accompanying accumulated depreciation as Leased Assets.

> **UNDERLYING CONCEPTS**
>
> Since the lessor owns the underlying asset, it depreciates the compactor over its entire useful life.

SPECIAL LEASE ACCOUNTING PROBLEMS

> **LEARNING OBJECTIVE 4**
> Discuss the accounting and reporting for special features of lease arrangements.

The features of lease arrangements that cause unique accounting problems are:

1. Residual values.

2. Other lease adjustments.

3. Bargain purchase options.

4. Short-term leases.

5. Presentation, disclosure, and analysis.

Residual Values

Lessee Perspective—Guaranteed Residual Value

In the Caterpillar/Sterling lease discussed earlier (on pages 21-11 to 21-15), the residual value was guaranteed by the lessee. This guaranteed residual value did not affect the computation of the lease liability, however, because it was probable that the expected residual value was greater than the guaranteed residual value. In other words, Sterling did not report a liability related to this guarantee because Sterling expects that it will not have to make a cash payment at the end of the lease. Sterling will simply return the backhoe to Caterpillar at the end of the lease.

The guidelines for accounting for a guaranteed residual value are as follows. [14]

1. If it is probable that the expected residual value is equal to or greater than the guaranteed residual value, the lessee should not include the guaranteed residual value in the computation of the lease liability.

2. If it is probable that the expected residual value is less than the guaranteed residual value, the difference between the expected and guaranteed residual values should be included in computation of the lease liability.

To illustrate a situation where the expected residual value is below the guaranteed residual value, assume in the earlier Caterpillar/Sterling example that it is probable that the residual value will be $3,000 instead of the guaranteed amount of $5,000. If Sterling estimates the residual value of the backhoe at the end of the lease to be $3,000, Sterling includes $2,000 ($5,000 − $3,000) as an additional lease payment in determining the lease liability and right-of-use asset. Illustration 21-21 shows the computation of the lease liability/right-of-use asset for Sterling in this situation.

ILLUSTRATION 21-21
Computation of Lessee's Capitalized Amount— Guaranteed Residual Value

STERLING'S CAPITALIZED AMOUNT (4% RATE)	
ANNUITY-DUE BASIS, INCLUDING GUARANTEED RESIDUAL VALUE	
Present value of five annual rental payments ($20,711.11 × 4.62990 (PVF-AD$_{5,4\%}$))	$95,890.35*
Present value of probable residual value payment of $2,000 due five years after date of commencement ($2,000 × .82193 (PVF$_{5,4\%}$))	1,643.86
Lessee's lease liability/right-of use asset	$97,534.21

*Rounded by $0.02.

ILLUSTRATION 21-22
Lease Amortization Schedule for Lessee— Guaranteed Residual Value

	STERLING CONSTRUCTION			
	LEASE AMORTIZATION SCHEDULE—GUARANTEED RESIDUAL VALUE			
	ANNUITY-DUE BASIS			
Date	Annual Lease Payment	Interest (4%) on Liability	Reduction of Lease Liability	Lease Liability
	(a)	(b)	(c)	(d)
1/1/17				$97,534.21
1/1/17	$ 20,711.11	$ -0-	$20,711.11	76,823.10
1/1/18	20,711.11	3,072.92	17,638.19	59,184.91
1/1/19	20,711.11	2,367.40	18,343.71	40,841.20
1/1/20	20,711.11	1,633.65	19,077.46	21,763.74
1/1/21	20,711.11	870.55	19,840.56	1,923.18
1/1/22	2,000.00	76.82*	1,923.18	0.00
	$105,555.55	$8,021.34	$97,534.21	

(a) Lease payment as required by lease.
(b) Four percent of the preceding balance of (d) except for 1/1/17; since this is an annuity due, no time has elapsed at the date of the first payment and therefore no interest has accrued.
(c) (a) minus (b).
(d) Preceding balance minus (c).

*Rounded by $0.11.

Sterling makes the following entries to record the lease and the first payment.

January 1, 2017

Right-of-Use Asset	97,534.21	
Lease Liability		97,534.21
(To record the right-of-use asset and related liability at commencement of the lease)		
Lease Liability	20,711.11	
Cash		20,711.11
(To record first lease payment)		

Sterling prepares a lease amortization schedule to show interest expense and related amortization of the lease liability over the five-year period. The schedule, shown in Illustration 21-22 (page 21-23), is based on an expected residual value payment of $2,000 ($5,000 − $3,000) at the end of five years.

Illustration 21-23 shows, in comparative form, Sterling's entries for the first two years of the lease when:

1. Sterling expects to pay $2,000 at the end of the lease related to the guaranteed residual value (see Illustration 21-22).

2. Sterling does not expect to owe an additional payment for the guaranteed residual value (see Illustration 21-8).

ILLUSTRATION 21-23
Journal Entries—Guaranteed Residual Value

Guaranteed Residual Value ($2,000 expected payment)		Guaranteed Residual Value (no expected payment)	
Capitalization of lease (January 1, 2017):			
Right-of-Use Asset	97,534.21	Right-of-Use Asset	95,890.35
Lease Liability	97,534.21	Lease Liability	95,890.35
First payment (January 1, 2017):			
Lease Liability	20,711.11	Lease Liability	20,711.11
Cash	20,711.11	Cash	20,711.11
Adjusting entry for accrued interest (December 31, 2017):			
Interest Expense	3,072.92	Interest Expense	3,007.17
Lease Liability	3,072.92	Lease Liability	3,007.17
Entry to record amortization of the ROU asset (December 31, 2017):			
Amortization Expense	19,506.84	Amortization Expense	19,178.07
Right-of-Use Asset ($97,534.21 ÷ 5 years)	19,506.84	Right-of-Use Asset ($95,890.35 ÷ 5 years)	19,178.07
Second payment (January 1, 2018):			
Lease Liability ($3,072.92 + $17,638.19)	20,711.11	Lease Liability ($3,007.17 + $17,703.94)	20,711.11
Cash	20,711.11	Cash	20,711.11

Following similar entries in subsequent years of the lease and using the amounts in Illustration 21-22, at the end of the lease term (January 1, 2022), Sterling returns the asset to Caterpillar and makes the following entries under the two situations.

Guaranteed Residual Value ($2,000 expected payment)		Guaranteed Residual Value (no expected payment)	
Final payment (January 1, 2022):			
Lease Liability	2,000.00	No entry	
Cash	2,000.00		

Following the entries summarized in Illustrations 21-23 and 21-24, the Right-of-Use Asset and the Lease Liability accounts have been fully amortized and have zero balances. If at the end of the lease (January 1, 2022) Sterling has no additional obligations under the residual value guarantee, no further entries are needed.

ILLUSTRATION 21-24
Final Payments—Guaranteed and Unguaranteed Residual Value

However, if the fair value of the underlying asset is less than the expected residual value, such that Sterling will have to further compensate Caterpillar under the residual value guarantee, Sterling will record a loss. For example, assume that due to poor maintenance of the backhoe, Sterling and Caterpillar agree that the fair value of the asset is sufficiently below the expected fair value such that Sterling must pay an additional $1,000 upon returning the backhoe to Caterpillar on January 1, 2022. In this case, Sterling reports a loss of $1,000, as reflected in the following journal entry.

January 1, 2022

Lease Liability	2,000	
Loss on Lease (Residual Value Guarantee)	1,000	
Cash		3,000

Lessee Perspective—Unguaranteed Residual Value

A lessee does not include an unguaranteed residual value in the computation of the lease liability, whether it is a finance lease or an operating lease. At the end of the lease, the lessee simply returns the leased asset to the lessor without any other payment. The Josway/Trayor example (on pages 21-18 to 21-22) illustrates the lessee accounting for an unguaranteed residual value.

Lessor Perspective—Guaranteed Residual Value

In the Sterling/Caterpillar example (on pages 21-11 to 21-15), Sterling guaranteed a residual value of $5,000. In computing the amount to be recovered from the rental payments, the present value of the residual value was subtracted from the fair value of the backhoe to arrive at the amount to be recovered by the lessor. Illustration 21-25 shows this computation.

ILLUSTRATION 21-25
Lease Payment Calculation

Amount to be recovered by lessor through lease payments	$95,890.35
Five beginning-of-year lease payments to earn a 4% return ($95,890.35 ÷ 4.62990 ($PVF\text{-}AD_{5,4\%}$))	$20,711.11

The computation in Illustration 21-25 is the same whether the residual value is guaranteed or unguaranteed.

The Caterpillar/Sterling lease agreement accounted for the lease as a sales-type lease. Caterpillar therefore recorded sales revenue and related cost of goods sold at lease commencement. Caterpillar accounts for the guaranteed residual value as part of sales revenue because the lessor receives this amount at the end of the lease either in cash or in the residual value returned.

Lessor Perspective—Unguaranteed Residual Value

What happens if the residual value for Caterpillar is unguaranteed? In this case, there is less certainty that the unguaranteed residual portion of the asset has been "sold." Therefore, the lessor recognizes sales revenue and cost of goods sold only for the portion of the asset for which recovery is assured. To account for this uncertainty, both sales revenue and cost of goods sold are reduced by the present value of the unguaranteed residual value. Given that the amount subtracted from sales revenue and cost of goods sold are the same, the gross profit computed will still be the same amount as when a guaranteed residual value exists.

To compare a sales-type lease with a guaranteed residual value to one with an unguaranteed residual value, assume the same facts as in the Caterpillar/Sterling lease situation (on page 21-12). That is:

1. The sales price is $100,000.

2. The expected residual value is $5,000 (the present value of which is $4,109.65).

3. The leased equipment has an $85,000 cost to the dealer, Caterpillar.

Illustration 21-26 shows the computation of the amounts relevant to a sales-type lease, under both a guaranteed and unguaranteed residual value situation.

	Guaranteed Residual Value	Unguaranteed Residual Value	
Lease receivable	$100,000 [$20,711.11 × 4.62990 (*PVF-AD*$_{5,4\%}$) + $5,000 × .82193 (*PVF*$_{5,4\%}$)]	Same	
Sales price of the asset	$100,000	$95,890.35 ($100,000 − $4,109.65)	
Cost of goods sold	$85,000	$80,890.35 ($85,000.00 − $4,109.65)	
Gross profit	$15,000 ($100,000 − $85,000)	$15,000 ($95,890.35 − $80,890.35)	

ILLUSTRATION 21-26
Computation of Lease Amounts by Caterpillar Financial—Sales-Type Lease

Caterpillar records the same gross profit ($15,000) at the point of sale whether the residual value is guaranteed or unguaranteed. However, the amounts recorded for sales revenue and the cost of goods sold are different between the guaranteed and unguaranteed situations. The reason for the difference is the uncertainty surrounding the realization of the unguaranteed residual value. Unlike the guaranteed residual value situation, where the lessor knows that it will receive the full amount of the guarantee at the end of the lease, in an unguaranteed residual value situation the lessor is not sure what it will receive at the end of the lease regarding the residual value. That is, due to the uncertainty surrounding the realization of the unguaranteed residual value, sales revenue and related cost of goods sold are reduced by the present value of the residual value. This results in **the sales revenue and cost of goods sold amounts being reported at different amounts under an unguaranteed residual value situation**.

Caterpillar makes the entries with respect to the lease arrangement under guaranteed and unguaranteed residual value situations (see pages 21-17 to 21-18), as shown in Illustration 21-27.

ILLUSTRATION 21-27
Entries for Guaranteed and Unguaranteed Residual Values—Sales-Type Lease

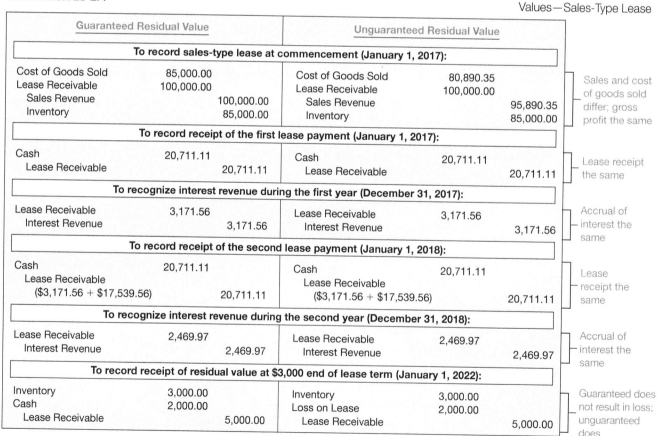

Guaranteed Residual Value			Unguaranteed Residual Value			
To record sales-type lease at commencement (January 1, 2017):						
Cost of Goods Sold	85,000.00		Cost of Goods Sold	80,890.35		Sales and cost of goods sold differ; gross profit the same
Lease Receivable	100,000.00		Lease Receivable	100,000.00		
Sales Revenue		100,000.00	Sales Revenue		95,890.35	
Inventory		85,000.00	Inventory		85,000.00	
To record receipt of the first lease payment (January 1, 2017):						
Cash	20,711.11		Cash	20,711.11		Lease receipt the same
Lease Receivable		20,711.11	Lease Receivable		20,711.11	
To recognize interest revenue during the first year (December 31, 2017):						
Lease Receivable	3,171.56		Lease Receivable	3,171.56		Accrual of interest the same
Interest Revenue		3,171.56	Interest Revenue		3,171.56	
To record receipt of the second lease payment (January 1, 2018):						
Cash	20,711.11		Cash	20,711.11		Lease receipt the same
Lease Receivable			Lease Receivable			
($3,171.56 + $17,539.56)		20,711.11	($3,171.56 + $17,539.56)		20,711.11	
To recognize interest revenue during the second year (December 31, 2018):						
Lease Receivable	2,469.97		Lease Receivable	2,469.97		Accrual of interest the same
Interest Revenue		2,469.97	Interest Revenue		2,469.97	
To record receipt of residual value at $3,000 end of lease term (January 1, 2022):						
Inventory	3,000.00		Inventory	3,000.00		Guaranteed does not result in loss; unguaranteed does
Cash	2,000.00		Loss on Lease	2,000.00		
Lease Receivable		5,000.00	Lease Receivable		5,000.00	

Illustration 21-28 (page 21-27) provides a summary of the accounting treatment for guaranteed and unguaranteed residual values by lessees and lessors related to the present value classification test and the measurement of the lease liability and receivable.

	Unguaranteed Residual Value	Guaranteed Residual Value		
LESSEE				
Classification Test	Ignore	Include full amount of residual value in present value test		
Measurement of Liability	Ignore	• If expected value of residual value >/= to guaranteed residual value, ignore • If expected value of residual value </= to guaranteed residual value, include the present value of the difference between the expected and guaranteed residual value in computation of lease liabilty		
LESSOR				
Classification Test	Ignore	Include		
Measurement of Receivable	Include	Include		

Note: When residual value is not guaranteed in a sales-type lease, lessor reduces Sales and Cost of Goods Sold by the present value of the unguaranteed residual value.

ILLUSTRATION 21-28
Summary of Treatment of Residual Values

Other Lease Adjustments

Additional lease adjustments that affect the measurement of lease assets and liabilities relate to the following:

1. Executory costs.

2. Lease prepayments and incentives.

3. Initial direct costs.

Executory Costs

Executory costs are normal expenses associated with owning a leased asset, such as property insurance and property taxes. The accounting for executory costs depends on how the lease is structured, that is, whether the lease is a gross lease or a net lease. In a gross lease, the payments to the lessor are fixed as part of the rental payments in the contract. In a net lease, the lessee makes variable payments to a third party or to the lessor directly for the executory costs. Illustration 21-29 provides examples of these two situations.

ILLUSTRATION 21-29
Executory Cost Example

GROSS VERSUS NET LEASES

Facts: Ortiz Company enters into a lease arrangement to lease a retail space in a shopping mall from Bryant Inc. The lease term is 2 years with monthly payments of $15,000 per month. Ortiz does not have any obligation to pay any of the property taxes or property insurance on the retail space. Ortiz estimates that Bryant is paying approximately $1,500 per month related to these executory costs.

Question: How should Ortiz account for the executory costs in this situation?

Solution: Ortiz and Bryant have a gross lease arrangement in that the property taxes and property insurance are included in the rental payments made by Ortiz. In this arrangement, the payment for the executory costs are fixed (per the rental agreement) and should be included in the computation of the lease liability.

Now assume that Ortiz agrees to a lease arrangement in which it must reimburse the lessor for the property taxes and property insurance, or pay a relevant third party directly. In this case, Ortiz and Bryant have a net lease arrangement because the lessee makes variable payments to a third party or to the lessor for the executory costs. In this case, Ortiz is responsible for paying directly the executory costs and therefore it is a variable payment which is expensed in the period incurred (not included in the lease liability and right-of-use assets).

Note that including executory costs in the measurement of the lease liability and related right-of-use asset may lead to inflated values on the balance sheet in comparison to lessees who do not capitalize these costs. Thus, the way parties structure the payment of executory costs (i.e., variable or fixed) can have potentially material implications with regard to the values that appear on the balance sheet.

In summary, executory costs included in the fixed payments required by the lessor should be included in lease payments for purposes of measuring the lease liability. Payments by the lessee made directly to the taxing authority or insurance provider are considered variable payments and are expensed as incurred. **[15]**

Lease Prepayments and Incentives

For all leases at the commencement date, the lease liability is the starting point to determine the amount to record for the right-of-use asset. Companies adjust the right-of-use asset for any lease prepayments, lease incentives, and initial direct costs made prior to or at the commencement date. These adjustments determine the amount to report as the right-of-use asset at the lease commencement date as follows.

1. Lease prepayments made by the lessee **increase** the right-of-use asset.
2. Lease incentive payments made by the lessor to the lessee **reduce** the right-of-use asset.
3. Initial direct costs incurred by the lessee (discussed in the next section) **increase** the right-of-use asset.

Illustration 21-30 identifies the adjustments made to the lease liability balance to determine the proper amount to report for the right-of-use asset.

Initial Measurement of Lease Liability	+	Prepaid Lease Payments	–	Lease Incentives Received	+	Initial Direct Costs	=	Right-of-Use Asset

ILLUSTRATION 21-30
Right-of-Use Asset Adjustments

Initial Direct Costs

Initial direct costs are incremental costs of a lease that would not have been incurred had the lease not been executed. **[16]** Costs directly or indirectly attributable to negotiating and arranging the lease (e.g., external legal costs to draft or negotiate a lease or an allocation of internal legal costs) are not considered initial direct costs. Illustration 21-31 provides examples of costs included and excluded from initial direct costs from the lessee and lessor side.[17]

Included	Excluded
• Commissions (including payments to employees acting as selling agents) • Legal fees resulting from the execution of the lease • Lease document preparation costs incurred after the execution of the lease • Consideration paid for a guarantee of residual value by an unrelated third party	• Employee salaries • Internal engineering costs • Legal fees for services rendered before the execution of the lease • Negotiating lease term and conditions • Advertising • Depreciation • Costs related to an idle asset

ILLUSTRATION 21-31
Initial Direct Costs

Initial direct costs incurred by the lessee are included in the cost of the right-of-use asset but are not recorded as part of the lease liability.

Illustration 21-32 provides an example of the computation of the right-of-use asset with initial direct costs.

For lessors, initial direct costs often are more significant because they are usually the party that solicits lessees as part of their sales activities. As a result, lessors often engage attorneys to prepare the legal documents, as well as pay commissions incurred in connection with the execution of a lease.

RIGHT–OF–USE COST ANALYSIS

ILLUSTRATION 21-32
Computation of Right–of-Use Asset

Facts: Mangan Company leases from DeMallie Co. solar equipment for 8 years starting on January 1, 2017. The lease is a finance/sales-type lease. The terms of the lease are as follows.

1. DeMallie will pay Mangan $30,000 as a cash incentive for entering the lease by January 1, 2017.
2. DeMallie pays initial direct costs of $5,000 for legal fees related to the execution of the lease.
3. Mangan incurred $1,500 of initial direct costs (commission paid to lease negotiator) which are payable by January 1, 2017.
4. Mangan must pay not only the first rental payment of $10,000 on January 1, 2018, but has to prepay the last month's rental payment on December 31, 2017.
5. The initial measurement of the liability is $400,000.

Question: What is the amount to be reported for Mangan's right-of-use asset at the commencement date?

---

[17] Adapted from PricewaterhouseCoopers, *Leases—2016* (*www.pwc.com*), p. 4-4.

ILLUSTRATION 21-32
Computation of
Right–of–Use Asset
(continued)

Solution: The measurement of the right-of-use asset for Mangan is as follows.	
Initial measurement of the lease liability	$400,000
Cash incentive received from DeMallie (lessor)	(30,000)
Initial direct costs (commission paid to lease negotiator)	1,500
Prepayments made by Mangan to DeMallie before the lease commencement	10,000
Measurement of right-of-use asset at January 1, 2017	$381,500

Mangan therefore reports the right-of-use asset at $381,500.

DeMaille (the lessor) expenses its initial direct costs in the period incurred, given DeMaille reported a gross profit related to its sale-type lease.

Lessor accounting for initial direct costs depends on the type of lease. **[17]**

- For **operating leases**, a lessor defers the initial direct costs and amortizes them as expenses over the term of the lease.
- For **sales-type leases**, the lessor expenses initial direct costs at lease commencement (in **the period** in which it recognizes the profit on the sale). An exception is when there is no selling profit or loss on the transaction. If there is no selling profit or loss, the initial direct costs are deferred and recognized over the lease term.

Lessors commonly also incur internal costs related to leasing activities. Examples are activities the lessor performs for advertising, servicing existing leases, and establishing and monitoring credit policies, as well as the costs for supervision and administration or for expenses such as rent and depreciation. Internal direct costs should not be included in initial direct costs. Such costs would have been incurred regardless of whether a lease was executed. As a result, internal direct costs are generally expensed as incurred.

Bargain Purchase Options

As stated earlier, a **bargain purchase option** allows the lessee to purchase the leased property for a future price that is substantially lower than the asset's expected future fair value. This price is so favorable at the lease's commencement that the future exercise of the option appears to be reasonably certain. If a bargain purchase option exists, **the lessee must increase the present value of the lease payments by the present value of the option price**.

For example, assume that Sterling Construction (see Illustration 21-22 on page 21-23) had an option to buy the leased equipment for $2,000 at the end of the five-year lease term. At that point, Sterling and Caterpillar expect the fair value to be $18,000. The significant difference between the option price and the fair value creates a bargain purchase option as the exercise of that option is reasonably certain.

A bargain purchase option affects the accounting for leases in the same way as a guaranteed residual value with a probable amount to be owed. In other words, with a guaranteed residual value, the lessee is expected to make an additional payment related to the residual value at the end of the lease. Similarly, the cost of a bargain purchase option is expected to be paid by the lessee. Therefore, the computations, amortization schedule, and entries prepared for this $2,000 bargain purchase option are identical to those shown for the $2,000 probable amount to be owed under the guaranteed residual value (see Illustrations 21-22, 21-23, and 21-24 on pages 21-23 and 21-24).

The only difference between the accounting treatment for a bargain purchase option and a guaranteed residual value of identical amounts and circumstances is in the **computation of the annual amortization**. In the case of a guaranteed residual value, Sterling amortizes the right-of-use asset over the lease term. In the case of a bargain purchase option, it uses the **economic life** of the underlying asset, given that the lessee takes ownership of the asset.

Short-Term Leases

A short-term lease is a **lease** that, at the **commencement date**, has a **lease term** of 12 months or less. Rather than recording a right-of-use asset and lease liability, lessees may elect to expense the lease payments as incurred. **[18]**

Leases may include options to either extend the term of the lease (a renewal option) or to terminate the lease prior to the contractually defined lease expiration date (a termination option). In these situations, renewal or termination options that are reasonably certain of exercise by the lessee are included in the lease term. Therefore, a one-year lease with a renewal option that the lessee is reasonably certain to exercise is not a short-term lease. Illustration 21-33 provides an example of two short-term lease situations.[18]

SHORT-TERM LEASES

Facts: (a) Thomas Company (lessee) enters into an arrangement to lease a crane for a 6-month period, with the option to extend the term for up to 9 additional months (in 3-month increments). After considering the nature of the project, Thomas determines that it expects to use the crane for only 9 months and is therefore reasonably certain that it will exercise only one of the 3-month renewal options.

(b) Thomas Company enters into the same arrangement as in part (a) but the project for which the crane is being used is now expected to take 15 months to complete. After considering the nature of the project, Thomas determines that it expects to use the crane for 15 months and is therefore reasonably certain that it will exercise all three renewal options.

Question: How would Thomas report these two situations?

Solutions: (a) Since the lease term is not more than 12 months, Thomas is able to elect the short-term lease exception because the lease term is not more than 12 months as it does not expect to exercise the renewal option.

(b) The expected lease term is greater than 12 months because Thomas expects to exercise all three renewal options. Thus, Thomas is not able to apply the short-term lease exception and must record a right-of-use asset and related lease liability.

ILLUSTRATION 21-33
Short-Term Lease Examples

Presentation, Disclosure, and Analysis

Presentation

Presented in Illustration 21-34 is a summary of how the **lessee** reports the information related to finance and operating leases in the financial statements.

	Balance Sheet	Income Statement
Finance Lease	Right-of-use asset Lease liability	Amortization expense Interest expense
Operating Lease	Right-of-use asset Lease liability	Lease expense

ILLUSTRATION 21-34
Presentation in Financial Statements—Lessee

Presented in Illustration 21-35 is a summary of **lessor** presentation of lease information in the financial statements.

	Balance Sheet	Income Statement
Sales-Type Lease	Lease receivable presented separate from other assets Derecognize the leased asset	Interest revenue Selling profit or loss
Operating Lease	Continue to recognize assets subject to operating leases as property, plant, and equipment	Revenue generally recognized on a straight-line basis Depreciation expense on the leased asset

ILLUSTRATION 21-35
Presentation in Financial Statements—Lessor

Disclosure

Lessees and lessors must also provide additional qualitative and quantitative disclosures to help financial statement users assess the amount, timing, and uncertainty of future cash flows. These disclosures are intended to supplement the amounts provided in the financial statements. Qualitative disclosures to be provided by both lessees and lessors are summarized in Illustration 21-36. **[19]**

- Nature of its leases, including general description of those leases.
- How variable lease payments are determined.
- Existence and terms and conditions for options to extend or terminate the lease and for residual value guarantees.
- Information about significant assumptions and judgments (e.g., discount rates).

ILLUSTRATION 21-36
Qualitative Lease Disclosures

[18]Adapted from PricewaterhouseCoopers, *Leases –2016* (*www.pwc.com*), Chapter 4.

Illustration 21-37 presents the type of quantitative information that should be disclosed for **the lessee**.

ILLUSTRATION 21-37
Lessee Quantitative
Disclosures

- Total lease cost.
- Finance lease cost, segregated between the amortization of the right-of-use assets and interest on the lease liabilities.
- Operating and short-term lease cost.
- Weighted-average remaining lease term and weighted-average discount rate (segregated between finance and operating leases).
- Maturity analysis of finance and operating lease liabilities, on an annual basis for a minimum of each of the next five years, the sum of the undiscounted cash flows for all years thereafter.

Illustration 21-38 presents a sample disclosure typical of a lessee having both finance leases and operating leases.

ILLUSTRATION 21-38
Lessee Sample Disclosure
Description of leased assets
Lease costs, segregation of finance, operating, and short-term lease costs
Weighted-average lease term
Weighted-average discount rate
Maturity analysis

Note 12:   Leases

The Company has long-term leases for stores and equipment. Aggregate minimum annual rentals at December 31, 2018 and 2017 under non-cancelable leases are as follows (dollar amounts in thousands):

	Year Ending December 31	
	2018	2017
Lease Cost		
Finance lease cost		
Amortization of right-of-use assets	$ 600	$ 525
Interest on lease liabilities	150	110
Operating lease cost	1,000	900
Short-term lease cost	50	40
Variable lease cost	75	60
Total lease cost	$1,875	$1,635
Other Information		
(Gains) and losses on sale and leaseback transactions, net	$ (8)	$ 5
Cash paid for amounts included in the measurement of lease liabilities for finance leases		
Operating cash flows	1,400	1,300
Financing cash flows	200	170
Cash paid for amounts included in the measurement of lease liabilities for operating leases		
Operating cash flows	800	635
Right-of-use assets obtained in exchange for new finance lease liabilities	475	515
Right-of-use assets obtained in exchange for new operating lease liabilities	150	175
Weighted-average remaining lease term—finance leases	9.7 years	2.9 years
Weighted-average remaining lease term—operating leases	5.2 years	5.4 years
Weighted-average discount rate—finance leases	5.8%	6.0%
Weighted-average discount rate—operating	6.1%	6.3%

Maturity Analysis

The Company has long-term leases for stores and equipment. Aggregate minimum annual rentals at December 31 under non-cancelable leases are as follows (dollar amounts in thousands):

	Operating	Finance
2019	$ 1,759	$ 504
2020	1,615	476
2021	1,482	444
2022	1,354	408
2023	1,236	370
Thereafter	10,464	3,252
Total payments	$17,910	$5,454

Illustration 21-39 shows the type of quantitative information that should be disclosed for **the lessor**.

ILLUSTRATION 21-39
Lessor Quantitative
Disclosures

- Lease-related income, including profit and loss recognized at lease commencement for sales-type and direct financing leases, and interest income.
- Income from variable lease payments not included in the lease receivable.
- The components of the net investment in sales-type and direct financing leases, including the carrying amount of the lease receivable, the unguaranteed residual asset, and any deferred profit on direct financing leases.
- A maturity analysis for operating lease payments and a separate maturity analysis for the lease receivable (sales-type and direct financing leases).
- Management approaches for risk associated with residual value of leased assets (e.g., buyback agreements or third-party insurance).

Illustration 21-40 provides a sample **lessor** disclosure.

ILLUSTRATION 21-40
Disclosure of Leases by
Lessor

Note 11: Sales-Type Lease Receivables and Operating Leases

Financing receivables represent sales-type leases resulting from the marketing of our products. These receivables typically have terms from two to five years and are usually collateralized by a security interest in the underlying assets. Financing receivables also include billed receivables from operating leases. The components of net financing receivables, which are included in financing receivables and long-term financing receivables and other assets, were as follows for the following fiscal years ended December 31:

Description of leased assets

	2018	2017
Lease Income		
Interest income	$ 612	$ 685
Gross profit on sales-type leases	2,645	2,813
Total lease-related income	$3,257	$3,498
Lease Receivables		
Minimum lease payments receivable	$6,982	$7,505
Allowance for doubtful accounts	(111)	(131)
Unguaranteed residual value	235	252
Unearned income	(547)	(604)
Financing receivables, net	6,559	7,022
Less current portion	(2,946)	(3,144)
Amounts due after one year, net	$3,613	$3,878

Lease income

Net investment

As of December 31, 2018, scheduled maturities of lease payments receivable were as follows for the following fiscal years ended December 31:

	2019	2020	2021	2022	2023	Thereafter	Total
Scheduled maturities of lease payments receivable	$3,220	$1,959	$1,112	$483	$174	$34	$6,982

Maturity analysis

Equipment leased to customers under operating leases was $4.0 billion at December 31, 2018 and $3.8 billion at December 31, 2017 and is included in machinery and equipment. Accumulated depreciation on equipment under lease was $1.4 billion at December 31, 2018 and $1.5 billion at December 31, 2017. As of December 31, 2018, future rentals on non-cancelable operating leases related to leased equipment were as follows for the following fiscal years ended December 31:

	2019	2020	2021	2022	2023	Thereafter	Total
Minimum future rentals on non-cancelable operating leases	$1,487	$958	$467	$156	$50	$6	$3,124

Analysis

Many companies that lease are likely to see their balance sheets grow substantially over the next few years as a result of implementing the new standard on leasing. Estimates as to its dollar impact on the assets and liabilities of companies vary, but it will be in the trillions of dollars. For example, here are the possible effects on the assets and liabilities for the following five companies (in millions) as a result of capitalizing lease assets and related liabilities: (1) Walgreens, $33,721; (2) AT&T, $31,047; (3) CVS Health, $27,282; (4) Wal-Mart Stores, $17,910; and FedEx Corporation, $16,385.

Some contend that "grossing up" the assets and liabilities on companies' balance sheets will not have any significant impact on analysis, based on information in the financial statements. Their rationale is that stockholders' equity does not change substantially, nor will net income. In addition, it is argued that users can determine the obligations that lessees are incurring by examining the notes to the financial statements.

These assertions are debatable. With the increase in the assets and liabilities as a result of the new standard, a number of financial metrics used to measure the profitability and solvency of companies will change, which could create challenges when performing financial analysis. On the profitability side, return on assets will decrease because a company's assets will increase, but net income will often be the same. Furthermore, analysts commonly focus on income subtotals, such as earnings before interest, taxes, and depreciation and amortization (EBIDTA), which likely will require some adjustments as companies amortize right-of-use assets. On the solvency side, the debt to equity ratio will increase, and the interest coverage ratio will decrease. In addition, recent studies indicate that using only note disclosures to determine lease obligations have understated their numerical impact.[19]

One thing is certain—the grossing up of the assets and liabilities related to lease arrangements will have significant consequences on the organizational, operational, and contractual side. Examples are:

YOU WILL WANT TO READ THE IFRS INSIGHTS ON PAGES 21-77 TO 21-83 For discussion of IFRS related to lease accounting.

1. States often levy taxes based on property amounts, which will now be higher.

2. Performance metrics to evaluate management may have to change for companies, particularly when growth rates in assets are used or returns on assets are used to measure performance.

3. Companies may have contracts with the government for which reimbursement is based on rent expense, which may change the compensation agreement.

4. Debt covenants might require revisions.

Given the pervasiveness and magnitude of the changes, it is not surprising that the FASB is permitting an extended implementation window to allow companies and users of financial statements to adapt to the new standard.

EVOLVING ISSUE   BRING IT ON!

As discussed in the opening story, the lease accounting rules will bring a significant amount of lease-related assets and liabilities onto lessee balance sheets. Recent estimates for the largest 100 U.S. companies put the number at over $539 billion. Most agree this is a good result—applying the "right-of-use" model will result in reporting more relevant and representationally faithful information about leasing arrangements, which is a big win for investors and creditors. As the chairperson of the IASB remarked, ". . . a financing, in the form of a loan to purchase an asset . . . then is recorded. Call it a lease and miraculously it does not show up in your books. In my book, if it looks like a duck, swims like a duck, and quacks like a duck, then it probably is a duck. So is the case with debt—leasing or otherwise."

At the same time, an analysis of the new rules and how they might impact the advantages of leasing presented in the following table suggests that many of the advantages of leases will remain after implementation of the new rules.

---

[19]Pepa Kraft, "Rating Agency Adjustment to GAAP Financial Statements and Their Effect on Ratings and Credit Spreads," *The Accounting Review* (March 2015), Vol. 90, No. 2, pp 641–674. In addition, a study by J.P. Morgan showed significant variation in the range of analysts' estimates of the underlying lease obligations under the new rules. See P. Elwin and S. C. Fernandes, "Leases on B/S from 2017? Retailers and Transport Will Be Hit Hard in Leverage Terms," *Global Equity Research*, J.P. Morgan Securities (May 17, 2013).

Reason for Leasing	Details	Status After Proposed New Rules Implemented
Funding source	Additional capital source, 100% financing, fixed rate, level payments, longer terms.	Still a major benefit versus a purchase—fixed rate, level payments—especially for smaller companies with limited sources of capital.
Low-cost capital	Low payments/rate due to tax benefits, residual and lessor's comparatively low cost of funds.	Still a benefit versus a loan.
Tax benefits	Lessee cannot use tax benefits and lease versus buy shows lease option offers lowest after tax cost.	Still a benefit.
Manage need for assets/ residual risk transfer	Lessee has flexibility to return asset.	Still a benefit.
Convenience	Quick and convenient financing process often available at point-of-sale.	Still a benefit.
Regulatory	Can help in meeting capital requirements.	Still a partial benefit if the capitalized amount is less than the cost of the asset as it is in many leases due to residuals assumed and tax benefits.
Accounting	Asset and liability off-balance-sheet.	Still a partial benefit if the capitalized amount is less than the cost of the asset as it is in many leases due to residuals assumed and tax benefits.

Source: Equipment Leasing & Finance Foundation, *2016 State of the Equipment Finance Industry Report.*

With the new standard scheduled to take effect in 2019, companies are encouraged to address the following areas to help make the lease accounting changes go smoothly and to retain the many business advantages of leasing.

1. *Inventory all equipment lease and rental contracts.* Knowing the amounts and nature of contractual obligations and terms of leases will enable understanding of accounting and tracking needs.

2. *Identify IT/software requirements.* To determine if the technology in place will meet the new standards, ask accounting software vendors how they plan to support the changes.

3. *Review debt covenants.* Although the lease accounting changes will have limited effect on debt covenants, discuss fully any implications with banks or creditors.

4. *Seek out industry expertise and counsel.* In addition to getting accounting expertise, consult with equipment finance providers. Providers have hands-on experience, informational resources, and advice on industry best practices to help assess the possible impact of the changes on current and future leasing needs.

5. *Enact a plan.* With the information gathered, start planning the budget and resources necessary for updates and systems changes to support the new rules.

While change may seem inconvenient at first glance, reexamining and assessing business processes to accommodate the lease accounting changes could reap advantages. For example, better information and controls can help enable better tracking and asset management, avoid redundancies, and allow companies to negotiate better lease terms in the future. That is, adopting new lease accounting can be a win for lessees as well as for investors and creditors.

Sources: M. Murphy, "The Big Number: $539 Billion," *Wall Street Journal* (January 16, 2016); Hans Hoogervorst, "Harmonisation and Global Economic Consequences," Public lecture at the London School of Economics (November 6, 2012); and R. Petta, "Telecom Industry Update: Benefits of Financing Remain with Lease Accounting Changes," *Knowledge, Leasing/Finance* (http://www.telecomreseller.com/2016/05/09/telecom-industry-update-benefits-of-financing-remain-with-lease-accounting-changes/).

APPENDIX 21A SALE-LEASEBACKS

In a sale-leaseback arrangement, a company (the seller-lessee) transfers an asset to another company (the buyer-lessor) and then leases that asset back from the buyer-lessor. For example, Darden Restaurants sold off its Red Lobster division to Golden Gate Capital (a private equity firm) for $2.1 billion recently and then leased these restaurants back from Golden Gate Capital. This transaction is shown in Illustration 21A-1.

LEARNING OBJECTIVE *5
Describe the lessee's accounting for sale-leaseback transactions.

ILLUSTRATION 21A-1
Sale-Leaseback

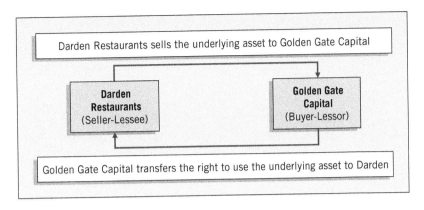

Why do companies like Darden Restaurants engage in sale-leaseback transactions? Some major reasons are:

1. Darden can use the cash that otherwise would be tied up in property to expand its operations. At the same time, it continues to use the property through the lease term.
2. Darden can structure the lease arrangement so issues such as repurchase provisions, refinancing issues, and conventional financing costs are minimized.
3. Darden may receive a tax advantage in that entire rental payments are tax-deductible, whereas under a conventional financing, only interest and depreciation can be deducted. If the lease has a significant land component (land is not depreciable) or if the fair value of the property is much greater than the carrying value of the property (depreciation limited to cost of property), then the sale lease-back arrangement generally reduces tax payments.

The advantages to Golden Gate Capital (buyer-lessor) are that it generally can earn a higher rate of return under a sale-leaseback than under traditional financing. In addition, during the lease term, Golden Gate is protected from a downturn in the real estate market and may have an inflation hedge, provided the property appreciates in value.

Sale-leasebacks are common and the dollar amounts related to these transactions are significant (approximately $15 billion per year). Financial institutions (e.g., Bank of America and First Chicago) have used this technique for their administrative offices, public utilities (e.g., Ohio Edison and Pinnacle West Corporation) for their generating plants, and airlines (such as Alaska Air Group) for their aircraft.

ACCOUNTING ISSUES IN SALE-LEASEBACK TRANSACTIONS

When Darden transferred the Red Lobster restaurants to Golden Gate Capital and then leased them back, the accounting issue is whether the transaction is a sale or a financing. To determine whether it is a sale, the revenue recognition guidelines are used. That is, if control has passed from seller to buyer, then a sale has occurred. Conversely, if control has not passed from seller to buyer, the transaction is recorded as a financing (often referred to as a failed sale). [20] Illustration 21A-2 highlights these two approaches.

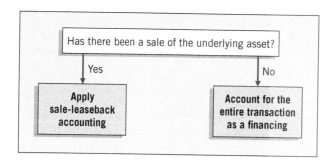

ILLUSTRATION 21A-2
Sale-Leaseback
Accounting

Sale Transaction

As indicated, if Darden (seller-lessee) **gives up control** of the Red Lobster restaurants, the transaction is a sale. In a sale, **gain or loss recognition** is appropriate. Darden then records the transaction as follows.

1. Increases cash and reduces the carrying value of the asset to zero (referred to as derecognizing the asset).
2. Recognizes a gain or loss as appropriate.
3. Accounts for the leaseback in accordance with lease accounting guidance used in this chapter.

For example, assume that Scott Paper sells one of its buildings having a carrying value of $580,000 (building $800,000 less accumulated depreciation $220,000) to General Electric for $623,110. It then leases the building back from General Electric for $50,000 a year, for eight of the building's 15 years of remaining economic life. Assume that the present value of these lease payments is equal to $310,000, such that the lease is classified as an operating lease. Scott Paper makes the following entries to record the sale-leaseback.

Cash	623,110	
Accumulated Depreciation—Buildings	220,000	
Buildings		800,000
Gain on Disposal of Plant Assets		43,110
($623,110 − $580,000)		

In addition, Scott makes an entry to record the operating lease from General Electric as follows.

Right-of-Use Asset	310,000	
Lease Liability		310,000

Financing Transaction (Failed Sale)

Scott Paper does not record a sale in the above transaction if the lease from General Electric is classified as a finance lease. The reason: if any of the lease classification tests are met, Scott, not General Electric, controls the asset. If Scott **continues to control the building, it should not record a sale nor recognize a gain or loss** on the transaction. In essence, Scott Paper is borrowing money from General Electric (often referred to as a financing or a failed sale). In a financing (failed sale), Scott:

- Does not reduce the carrying value of the building.
- Continues to depreciate the building as if it was the legal owner.
- Recognizes the sale proceeds from General Electric as a financial liability.

UNDERLYING CONCEPTS

A sale-leaseback under a financing transaction is similar in substance to the parking of inventories (discussed in Chapter 8). The ultimate economic benefits remain under the control of the "seller-lessee," so revenue (gain) should not be recognized.

The entry to record the financing is as follows.

Cash	623,110	
Notes Payable		623,110

SALE-LEASEBACK EXAMPLE

To illustrate the accounting treatment accorded a sale-leaseback transaction over the lease term, assume that American Airlines on January 1, 2017, sells a used, standard-design Boeing 757 having a carrying amount on its books of $30,000,000 to CitiCapital for $33,000,000. American immediately leases the aircraft back under the following conditions.

- The term of the lease is seven years. The lease agreement is non-cancelable, requiring equal rental payments of $4,881,448 at the end of each year (ordinary annuity basis), beginning December 31, 2017.

- The lease contains no renewal or purchase options. The plane reverts to CitiCapital at the termination of the lease.

- The aircraft has a fair value of $33,000,000 on January 1, 2017, and an estimated remaining economic life of 10 years. The residual value (unguaranteed) at the end of the lease is $13,000,000.

- The annual payments assure the lessor an 8 percent return (which is the same as American's incremental borrowing rate).

Applying the classification tests, the lease-back of the airplane is classified as an operating lease because none of the sales-type lease criteria are met, as indicated in Illustration 21A-3.

ILLUSTRATION 21A-3
Lease Classification Tests

Test	Assessment
1. Transfer of ownership test	Transfer of ownership does not occur; the asset reverts to CitiCapital at the end of the lease.
2. Purchase option test	There is no purchase option in the lease.
3. Lease term test	The lease term is 70 percent (7 ÷ 10) of the remaining economic life of the asset, which is less than the major part of the life of the asset (75 percent).
4. Present value test	The present value of the lease payments is $25,414,625*, which is 77 percent ($25,414,625 ÷ $33,000,000) of the fair value of the aircraft, or less than 90 percent. Therefore, the lease does not meet the present value test.
5. Alternative use test	As indicated, the equipment is not of a specialized nature and is expected to have use to CitiCapital when returned at the end of the lease.

*$4,881,448 × 5.20637 ($PVF\text{-}OA_{7,8\%}$)

Thus, this arrangement is accounted for as a sale, rather than a failed sale, because the leaseback does not transfer control of the asset back to American; that is, only the right-of-use for seven years is granted through the lease. Illustration 21A-4 presents the typical journal entries to record the sale-leaseback transactions for American and CitiCapital for the first two years of the lease.

As indicated, under the operating method, American amortizes the lease liability and right-of-use asset, resulting in straight-line expense recognition. CitiCapital (the buyer-lessor) continues to recognize the asset on its balance sheet and recognizes equal amounts of rental revenue (straight-line basis) in each period. It **depreciates the leased asset generally on a straight-line basis.**

American Airlines (Lessee)			CitiCapital (Lessor)		
Sale of aircraft by American to CitiCapital (January 1, 2017):					
Cash	33,000,000		Aircraft	33,000,000	
Gain on Disposal of Plant Assets		3,000,000	Cash		33,000,000
Aircraft		30,000,000			
Right-of-Use Asset	25,414,625				
Lease Liability		25,414,625			
First lease payment (December 31, 2017):					
Lease Expense ($2,033,170 + $2,848,278)	4,881,448		Cash	4,881,448	
Lease Liability (Schedule A)	2,848,278		Lease Revenue		4,881,448
Right-of-Use Asset (Schedule B)		2,848,278			
Cash		4,881,448			
Depreciation expense on the aircraft (December 31, 2017):					
No entry			Depreciation expense		
			($33,000,000 ÷ 10)	3,300,000	
			Accumulated Depreciation		
			– Leased Equipment		3,300,000
Second lease payment (December 31, 2018):					
Lease Expense ($1,805,308 + $3,076,140)	4,881,448		Cash	4,881,448	
Lease Liability	3,076,140		Lease Revenue		4,881,448
Right-of-Use Asset		3,076,140			
Cash		4,881,448			
Depreciation expense on the aircraft (December 31, 2018):					
No entry			Depreciation expense	3,300,000	
			($33,000,000 ÷ 10)		
			Accumulated Depreciation—		3,300,000
			Leased Equipment		

Schedule A: Partial Lease Amortization Schedule

Date	Annual Lease Payment	Interest (8%) on Liability	Reduction of Lease Liability	Lease Liability
Jan. 2017				$25,414,625
Dec. 2017	$4,881,448	$2,033,170	$2,848,278	22,566,347
Dec. 2018	4,881,448	1,805,308	3,076,140	19,490,207

Schedule B: Partial Lease Expense Schedule

Date	(A) Lease Expense (Straight-Line)	(B) Interest (8%) on Liability	(C) Amortization of ROU Asset (A – B)	(D) Carrying Value of ROU Asset (D – C)
Jan. 2017				$25,414,625
Dec. 2017	$4,881,448	$ 2,033,170	$2,848,278	22,566,347
Dec. 2018	4,881,448	1,805,308	3,076,140	19,490,207

ILLUSTRATION 21A-4
Comparative Entries for Sale-Leaseback for Lessee and Lessor

APPENDIX 21B   DIRECT FINANCING LEASE (LESSOR)

Lessors account for a lease as a sales-type lease if the lease transfers control of the underlying asset to the lessee, based on meeting one of the lease classification tests presented in Illustration 21-2 (on page 21-8). Leases that do not meet any of the classification tests are generally recorded as operating leases. However, lessors use a third lease classification—

LEARNING OBJECTIVE ˙6
Describe the lessor's accounting for a direct financing lease.

a direct financing lease—in one special situation. This situation occurs when the lessor **relinquishes control of the asset** to the lessee but there is also involvement of a third party. **[21]** This situation is common when a third-party residual value guarantee is involved. Illustration 21B-1 illustrates the decision process for direct financing lease classification.

ILLUSTRATION 21B-1
Direct Financing Lease
Classification

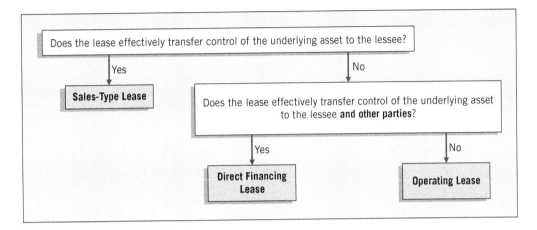

For example, in the Josway/Traylor compactor lease (on pages 21-18 to 21-22), both parties classified the lease as an operating lease because none of the transfer of control criteria were met. A condition of that agreement was that the residual value was not guaranteed by the lessee. It turns out that if the residual value was guaranteed by Traylor, the 90% test would be met and Josway and Traylor would account for this lease as a finance (sales-type) lease. However if Josway (the lessor) obtains the **residual value guarantee from a third party, Josway (the lessor) classifies the lease as a direct financing lease, not a sales-type lease.**[20]

DIRECT FINANCING LEASE ACCOUNTING

The basic difference between a direct financing lease and a sales-type lease relates to the profit on the sale. In a sales-type lease, the profit is recognized immediately. **In a direct financing lease, the profit is deferred and recognized over the life of the lease.**[21]

This accounting—with no selling profit recognized at the commencement of a direct financing lease—aligns with revenue recognition criteria because the lease does not transfer complete control of the underlying asset to the lessee. However, the lessor transfers substantially all the risks and rewards of ownership through the right-of-use of the underlying asset to one or more third parties. That is, in a direct financing lease, **the presence of a third-party guarantee effectively converts the lessor's risk arising from the underlying asset into a credit risk.** Given that the lessor now has credit risk, the FASB concluded that the lessor should not be permitted to recognize gross profit on the lease at the commencement of the lease. Instead, the lessor should defer the profit and recognize this profit over the life of the lease arrangement.[22] **[23]**

DIRECT FINANCING LEASE EXAMPLE

Assume that Ormand Company (the lessor) enters into a lease agreement with Amazon.com for the use of one of Ormand's standard motorized warehouse package pickers. Information relevant to the lease is as follows (page 21-40).

---

[20]For classification as a direct financing lease, it must be probable that the lessor will collect the lease payments and any amounts related to the residual value guarantee(s).

[21]Losses at commencement of a direct financing lease are recognized immediately. **[22]**

[22]In addition, lessor initial direct costs are deferred and amortized over the life of the lease.

- The lease commencement date is January 1, 2017, with a term of three years. The lease agreement is non-cancelable, requiring equal rental payments at the end of each year (ordinary annuity).

- The picker has a fair value at commencement of the lease of $30,000 and a carrying value of $28,000, with an estimated residual value of $6,000 at the end of the lease. The picker has an estimated economic life of five years. Amazon provides a **guarantee that the residual value of the picker will be at least $6,000 at the end of the lease.**

- The lease contains no renewal options, and the picker reverts to Ormand at the termination of the lease.

- Ormand sets the annual rental rate to earn a rate of return of 6 percent per year (implicit rate) on its investment, as shown in Illustration 21B-2.

Fair value of leased equipment	$30,000.00
Less: Present value of the residual value ($6,000 × .83962 $(PVF_{3,6\%})$)	5,037.72
Amount to be recovered by lessor through lease payments	$24,962.28
Three end-of-year lease payments to earn a 6% return ($24,962.28 ÷ 2.67301 $(PVF\text{-}OA_{3,6\%})$)	$ 9,338.64

ILLUSTRATION 21B-2
Computation of Lease Payments

Evaluation of the classification tests, based on these facts, indicates that this lease is classified as a sales-type lease for Ormand because the present value test is met, as indicated in Illustration 21B-3.

Test	Assessment
1. Transfer of ownership test	Transfer of ownership does not occur; the asset reverts to Ormand at the end of the lease.
2. Purchase option test	There is no purchase option in the lease.
3. Lease term test	The lease term is 60 percent (3 ÷ 5) of the economic life of the asset, which is less than the major part of the life of the asset (75 percent).
4. Present value test	The present value of the lease payments is $30,000.00*, which is 100 percent ($30,000 ÷ $30,000, which is greater than or equal to 90 percent) of the fair value of the picker. Therefore, **the lease meets the present value test**.
5. Alternative use test	As indicated, the equipment is not of a specialized nature and is expected to have use to Ormand when returned at the end of the lease.

ILLUSTRATION 21B-3
Lease Classification Tests

*Present value of rental payments plus residual value guarantee discounted at 6%:

Present value of five annual rental payments ($9,338.64 × 2.67301 $(PVF\text{-}OA_{3,6\%})$)	$24,962.28
Present value of guaranteed residual value of $6,000 at end of the lease ($6,000 × .83962 $(PVF_{3,6\%})$)	5,037.72
	$30,000.00

Note that the residual value guarantee is provided by the lessee and therefore is included in the lease payments used in the present value test for classification purposes. Ormand accounts for the lease as a sale-type lease, recording a lease receivable and reducing the carrying value of the underlying asset (Inventory) to zero.

For a sales-type lease, Ormond makes the following journal entry at the beginning of the lease.

Lease Receivable	30,000	
Cost of Goods Sold	28,000	
Sales Revenue		30,000
Inventory		28,000

On January 1, 2017, Ormand therefore reports gross profit on the sale of the package picker of $2,000 ($30,000 − $28,000). In subsequent periods, Ormond reduces the lease receivable by the payments received and recognizes interest revenue using the 6 percent implicit rate.

On the other hand, if the residual value is **guaranteed by an unrelated third party, the lessor classifies the lease as a direct financing lease.** Ormand uses the direct financing method because, as discussed earlier, the lessor still maintains some control of the asset. That is, as a result of a third-party guarantee, the lessor does not effectively transfer all risks and rewards (control) of the underlying asset (until all residual value guarantees are satisfied). In this situation, and consistent with other revenue recognition concepts, sales revenue and related cost of goods sold are not recognized. Instead Ormond recognizes a deferred gross profit of $2,000, which is the difference between the fair value of the property ($30,000) and the carrying amount of the asset ($28,000). This deferred gross profit reduces the lease receivable in the lease, as shown in Illustration 21B-4 for the Ormand/Amazon lease.

ILLUSTRATION 21B-4
Net Investment, Direct Financing Lease

Lease Receivable	−	Deferred Gross Profit	=	Net Lease Receivable
$30,000	−	$2,000	=	$28,000

On January 1, 2017, Ormond makes the following entry to record the direct financing lease.

January 1, 2017

Lease Receivable	30,000	
Deferred Gross Profit		2,000
Inventory		28,000

Subsequent accounting for the direct financing lease is based on a discount rate that will amortize the net lease receivable to zero over the life of the lease. That is, in a direct financing lease, the rate used to amortize the lower net lease receivable (lease receivable less deferred gross profit) will be higher. This results because the rate includes interest revenue on the lease receivable and revenue from amortizing deferred gross profit. In other words, consider the following.

1. In a normal sale, Ormand would receive lease payments over the life of the lease which, on a present value basis, equals the lease receivable of $30,000 (a 6% rate of return). Interest on the lease receivable over the life of the lease is therefore $4,015.92. This computation is shown in Illustration 21B-5.

ILLUSTRATION 21B-5
Sale-Type Lease Amortization

	ORMAND COMPANY			
	SALES-TYPE LEASE AMORTIZATION SCHEDULE			
	ORDINARY ANNUITY BASIS			
Date	Annual Lease Payment	Interest (6%) on Receivable	Reduction of Lease Receivable	Lease Receivable
	(a)	(b)	(c)	(d)
1/1/17				$30,000.00
12/31/17	$ 9,338.64	$1,800.00	$ 7,538.64	22,461.36
12/31/18	9,338.64	1,347.68	7,990.96	14,470.40
12/31/19	9,338.64	868.24*	8,470.40	6,000.00
12/31/19	6,000.00	−0−	6,000.00	0.00
	$34,015.92	$4,015.92	$30,000.00	

(a) Lease payment as required by lease.
(b) Six percent of the preceding balance of (d).
(c) (a) minus (b).

*Rounded by $0.02.

2. In a direct financing arrangement, Ormand receives the same lease payments, which on a present value basis equals $28,000 (a 9.5% rate of return).[23] This computation is shown in Illustration 21B-6.

[23] The 9.5% rate is determined through trial and error or with a financial calculator to arrive at a discount rate for present values of the residual value (single sum) and payments (annuity), such that the net lease receivable, including the deferred gross profit, is amortized to zero (given the lease payments, as computed on the lease receivable of $30,000 and a 6% rate).

ORMAND COMPANY
DIRECT FINANCING LEASE AMORTIZATION SCHEDULE
ORDINARY ANNUITY BASIS

Date	Annual Lease Payment	Interest (9.5%) on Receivable	Reduction of Net Lease Receivable	Net Lease Receivable
	(a)	(b)	(c)	(d)
1/1/17				$28,000.00
12/31/17	$ 9,338.64	$2,660.00	$ 6,678.64	21,321.36
12/31/18	9,338.64	2,025.53	7,313.11	14,008.25
12/31/19	9,338.64	1,330.39*	8,008.25	6,000.00
12/31/19	6,000.00		6,000.00	0.00
	$34,015.92	$6,015.92	$28,000.00	

(a) Lease payment as required by lease.
(b) 9.5 percent of the preceding balance of (d).
(c) (a) minus (b).
(d) Preceding balance minus (c).
*Rounded by $0.39

As shown in Illustration 21B-6, Ormand then records Lease Revenue based on a discount rate of 9.5 percent applied to the net lease receivable balance. In this case, the revenue on the lease receivable is $6,015.92, which is $2,000 ($6,015.92 − $4,015.92) higher than under Illustration 21B-5. The difference results because the total lease revenue each year of the lease is comprised of interest revenue on the lease receivable plus the recognition of a portion of deferred gross profit. Ormand makes the following entry in 2017, based on the amounts presented in Illustration 21B-6.[24]

December 31, 2017

Cash	9,338.64	
Deferred Gross Profit ($2,660 − $1,800)	860.00	
Lease Revenue		2,660.00
Lease Receivable		7,538.64

Ormand reports the following information related to the direct financing lease at December 31, 2017, either in the balance sheet or notes to the financial statements, as shown in Illustration 21B-7.

Leases		
Lease receivable ($30,000.00 − $7,538.64)		$22,461.36
Less: Deferred gross profit ($2,000 − $860)		1,140.00
Net lease receivable		$21,321.36

[24]The reduction in deferred gross profit each year equals the difference in yearly amounts of interest revenue at 6% and 9.5%, as shown in column (b) of Illustrations 21B-5 and Illustration 21B-6, as indicated in the following table.

Date	Interest (6%) on Receivable	Lease Revenue (9.5%)	Reduction in Deferred Gross Profit	Deferred Gross Profit Balance
	(a)	(b)	(b) − (a)	
1/1/17				$2,000.00
12/31/17	$1,800.00	$2,660.00	$860.00	1,140.00
12/31/18	1,347.68	2,025.53	677.85	462.15
12/31/19	868.24	1,330.39	462.15	0

A Lease Revenue account is used because both defered gross profit and interest are recognized.

Ormand makes the following entries for payments in 2018 and 2019.

December 31, 2018

Cash	9,338.64	
Deferred Gross Profit ($2,025.53 − $1,347.68)	677.85	
Lease Revenue		2,025.53
Lease Receivable		7,990.96

December 31, 2019

Cash	9,338.64	
Deferred Gross Profit ($1,330.39 − $868.24)	462.15	
Lease Revenue		1,330.39
Lease Receivable		8,470.40

After the entry on December 31, 2019, to recognize interest revenue, Lease Receivable has a balance of $6,000, which equals the guaranteed residual value (the deferred gross profit has been fully amortized).

Assuming the underlying asset has a fair value of $6,000 at the end of the lease, Ormand makes the following entry.[25]

December 31, 2019

Inventory	6,000.00	
Lease Receivable		6,000.00

APPENDIX 21C   COMPREHENSIVE EXAMPLE

LEARNING OBJECTIVE *7
Apply lessee and lessor accounting to finance and operating leases.

This appendix presents a comprehensive illustration of lessee and lessor accounting for a lease arrangement when classified as a finance/sales-type or operating lease.

LEASE TERMS: SCENARIO 1

Parker Shipping Co. (lessee) leases a standard hydraulic lift from Stoughton Trailers Inc. (the lessor) that will be installed at one of Parker's loading docks. The lease, signed on January 1, 2017, specifies that Stoughton grants right-of-use of the lift to Parker under the following terms:

- The lease agreement is non-cancelable with a term of four years, requiring equal rental payments of $11,182.24 at the beginning of each year of the lease (annuity-due basis).

- The lift has a fair value at commencement of the lease of $40,000, an **estimated economic life of four years, and no residual value**. The cost of the lift on Stoughton's books is $30,000.

- The lease contains no renewal options. The lift reverts to Stoughton at the termination of the lease.

- The implicit rate of the lessor is 8 percent and is known by Parker. Stoughton sets the annual rental as shown in Illustration 21C-1.

---

[25]If the fair value of the leased asset is less than $6,000—e.g., $5,000 upon return—Ormand receives $1,000 from the third-party guarantor to compensate for the decline in the value of the asset below the guaranteed residual value. If the asset returned has a fair value in excess of $6,000, Ormand records the asset at the carrying amount of the residual value, and the gain is unrealized until the asset is sold.

Fair value of leased equipment	$40,000.00
Less—present value of the residual value	0.00
Amount to be recovered by lessor through lease payments	$40,000.00
Four beginning-of-year lease payments to earn an 8% return ($40,000 ÷ 3.57710 ($PVF\text{-}AD_{4,8\%}$))	$11,182.24

ILLUSTRATION 21C-1
Lease Payment Calculation

Lease Classification

The lease is classified as a finance/sales-type lease by Parker/Stoughton, as indicated by the analysis in Illustration 21C-2.

Test	Assessment
1. Transfer of ownership test	Transfer of ownership does not occur; the asset reverts to Stoughton at the end of the lease.
2. Purchase option test	There is no bargain purchase option in the lease.
3. Lease term test	The lease term is equal to the economic life of the asset (100 percent). Therefore, **the lease meets the lease term test**.
4. Present value test	The present value of the lease payments is $40,000*, which is 100 percent (greater than or equal to 90 percent) of the fair value of the hydraulic lift. Therefore, **the lease meets the present value test**.
5. Alternative use test	As indicated, the hydraulic lift will be completely used up at the end of the lease; it will not have use to Stoughton at the end of the lease.

*$11,182.24 × 3.57710 ($PVF\text{-}AD_{4,8\%}$) = $40,000.00

ILLUSTRATION 21C-2
Lease Classification Tests

Thus, the lease is classified as a finance/sales-type lease due to meeting the lease term and present value tests (either is sufficient).

Accounting for Finance Lease

The accounting for the lease liability (Parker) and lease receivable (Stoughton) is based on the amounts reported in the amortization schedule presented in Illustration 21C-3.[26]

PARKER SHIPPING/STOUGHTON TRAILERS
LEASE AMORTIZATION SCHEDULE
ANNUITY-DUE BASIS

Date	Annual Lease Payment	Interest (8%) on Liability/ Receivable	Reduction of Lease Liability/ Receivable	Lease Liability/ Receivable
	(a)	(b)	(c)	(d)
1/1/17				$40,000.00
1/1/17	$11,182.24	$ —	$11,182.24	28,817.76
1/1/18	11,182.24	2,305.42	8,876.82	19,940.94
1/1/19	11,182.24	1,595.28	9,586.96	10,353.98
1/1/20	11,182.24	828.26*	10,353.98	0.00
	$44,728.96	$4,728.96	$40,000.00	

(a) Lease payment as required by lease.
(b) Eight percent of the preceding balance of (d) except for 1/1/17; since this is an annuity due, no time has elapsed at the date of the first payment and therefore no interest has accrued.
(c) (a) minus (b).
(d) Preceding balance minus (c).
*Rounded by $0.06.

ILLUSTRATION 21C-3
Lease Liability Amortization Schedule

Entries for Parker (lessee) and Stoughton (lessor) over the life of the lease are presented in Illustration 21C-4 (on page 21-45), based on the amounts reported in the amortization schedule in Illustration 21C-3.

---

[26]The same amortization schedule can be used for the lessee and lessor because there is no residual value and Parker knows the implicit rate used by the lessor is setting the payments.

Parker Shipping (Lessee)		Stoughton Trailers (Lessor)	

Lease commencement/first payment (January 1, 2017):

Parker Shipping (Lessee)		Stoughton Trailers (Lessor)	
Right-of-Use Asset	40,000.00	Lease Receivable	40,000.00
Lease Liability	40,000.00	Cost of Goods Sold	30,000.00
		Inventory	30,000.00
		Sales Revenue	40,000.00
Lease Liability	11,182.24	Cash	11,182.24
Cash	11,182.24	Lease Receivable	11,182.24

Interest accrual and amortization expense (December 31, 2017):

Parker Shipping (Lessee)		Stoughton Trailers (Lessor)	
Interest Expense	2,305.42	Lease Receivable	2,305.42
Lease Liability	2,305.42	Interest Revenue	2,305.42
Amortization Expense	10,000.00	No entry	
Right-of-Use Asset ($40,000 ÷ 4 years)	10,000.00		

Balance Sheet		Income Statement		Balance Sheet		Income Statement	
Noncurrent assets		Interest expense	$ 2,305.42	Current assets		Sales revenue	$40,000.00
Right-of-use assets	$30,000.00	Amortization		Lease receivable	$11,182.24	Cost of goods sold	30,000.00
Current liabilities		expense	10,000.00	Noncurrent assets		Interest revenue	2,305.42
Lease liability	11,182.24			Lease receivable	19,940.94		
Noncurrent liabilities							
Lease liability	19,940.94						

Second lease payment (January 1, 2018):

Parker Shipping (Lessee)		Stoughton Trailers (Lessor)	
Lease Liability ($8,876.82 + $2,305.42)	11,182.24	Cash	11,182.24
Cash	11,182.24	Lease Receivable	11,182.24

Interest accrual and amortization expense (December 31, 2018):

Parker Shipping (Lessee)		Stoughton Trailers (Lessor)	
Interest Expense	1,595.28	Lease Receivable	1,595.28
Lease Liability	1,595.28	Interest Revenue	1,595.28
Amortization Expense	10,000.00	No entry	
Right-of-Use Asset ($40,000 ÷ 4 years)	10,000.00		

Balance Sheet		Income Statement		Balance Sheet		Income Statement	
Noncurrent assets		Interest expense	$ 1,595.28	Current assets		Interest revenue	$1,595.28
Right-of-use assets	$20,000.00	Amortization		Lease receivable	$11,182.24		
Current liabilities		expense	10,000.00	Noncurrent assets			
Lease liability	11,182.24			Lease receivable	10,353.98		
Noncurrent liabilities							
Lease liability	10,353.98						

Third lease payment (January 1, 2019):

Parker Shipping (Lessee)		Stoughton Trailers (Lessor)	
Lease Liability ($9,586.96 + $ 1,595.28)	11,182.24	Cash	11,182.24
Cash	11,182.24	Lease Receivable	11,182.24

Interest accrual and amortization expense (December 31, 2019):

Parker Shipping (Lessee)		Stoughton Trailers (Lessor)	
Interest Expense	828.26	Lease Receivable	828.26
Lease Liability	828.26	Interest Revenue	828.26
Amortization Expense	10,000.00	No entry	
Right-of-Use Asset ($40,000 ÷ 4 years)	10,000.00		

Balance Sheet		Income Statement		Balance Sheet		Income Statement	
Noncurrent assets		Interest expense	$ 828.26	Current assets		Interest revenue	$828.26
Right-of-use assets	$10,000.00	Amortization		Lease receivable	$11,182.24		
Current liabilities		expense	10,000.00				
Lease liability	$11,182.24						

Fourth lease payment (January 1, 2020):

Parker Shipping (Lessee)		Stoughton Trailers (Lessor)	
Lease Liability ($10,353.98 + $ 828.26)	11,182.24	Cash	11,182.24
Cash	11,182.24	Lease Receivable	11,182.24

ILLUSTRATION 21C-4
Lessee/Lessor Entries for
Finance/Sales-Type Lease

LEASE TERMS: SCENARIO 2

Now consider the following revised terms of the lease between Parker Shipping Co. and Stoughton Trailers Inc. for the right-of-use of a hydraulic lift. The lease, signed on January 1, 2017, specifies that Stoughton grants right-of-use of the lift to Parker under the following terms.

- The lease agreement is non-cancelable with a term of four years, requiring equal rental payments of $9,538.39 with the first payment on January 1, 2017 (annuity-due basis).

- The lift has a fair value at commencement of the lease of $40,000, an estimated **economic life of six years**. The lift has **a residual value** at the end of the lease of **$8,000 (unguaranteed).** The cost of the lift on Stoughton's books is $30,000.

- The lease contains no renewal options. The lift reverts to Stoughton at the termination of the lease.

- The implicit rate of Stoughton (the lessor) is 8 percent and is known by Parker.

Stoughton determines the rental payments such that it earns a rate of return of 8 percent per year (implicit rate) on its investment, as shown in Illustration 21C-5.

Fair value of leased equipment	$40,000.00
Less: Present value of the residual value ($8,000 × .73503($PV_{4,8\%}$))	5,880.24
Amount to be recovered by lessor through lease payments	$34,119.76
Four beginning-of-year lease payments to earn an 8% return ($34,119.76 ÷ 3.57710 ($PVF\text{-}AD_{4,8\%}$))	$ 9,538.39

ILLUSTRATION 21C-5
Computation of Lease Payments

Lease Classification

The lease is classified as an operating lease by Parker and Stoughton, as indicated by the analysis in Illustration 21C-6.

Test	Assessment
1. Transfer of ownership test	Transfer of ownership does not occur; the asset reverts to Stoughton at the end of the lease.
2. Purchase option test	There is no bargain purchase option in the lease.
3. Lease term test	The lease term is 66.67 percent (4 ÷ 6) of the economic life of the asset, which is less than the major part of the life of the asset (75 percent).
4. Present value test	The present value of the lease payments is $34,119.76*, which is 85.3 percent ($34,119.76 ÷ $40,000) of the fair value of the lift. Therefore, it does not meet the present value test.
5. Alternative use test	As indicated, the equipment is not of a specialized nature and is expected to have use to Stoughton when returned at the end of the lease.

*$9,538.39 × 3.57710 ($PVF\text{-}AD_{4,8\%}$)

ILLUSTRATION 21C-6
Lease Classification Tests

Thus, the lease is classified as an operating lease by both the lessee and lessor, as none of the classification tests are met.

Lessee Accounting—Operating Lease

Parker makes the following entry to record this operating lease and the first payment.

January 1, 2017

Right-of-Use Asset	34,119.76	
Lease Liability		34,119.76
(To record right-of-use asset and related liability)		
Lease Liability	9,538.39	
Cash		9,538.39
(To record first payment)		

Illustration 21C-7 shows the interest expense and amortization of the lease liability, applying the effective-interest method.

ILLUSTRATION 21C-7
Lease Amortization
Schedule

	PARKER SHIPPING CO.			
	LEASE AMORTIZATION SCHEDULE			
	ANNUITY-DUE BASIS			
Date	Annual Lease Payment	Interest (8%) on Liability	Reduction of Lease Liability	Lease Liability
	(a)	(b)	(c)	(d)
1/1/17				$34,119.76
1/1/17	$ 9,538.39	$ -0-	9,538.39	24,581.37
1/1/18	9,538.39	1,966.51	7,571.88	17,009.49
1/1/19	9,538.39	1,360.76	8,177.63	8,831.86
11/1/20	9,538.39	706.53*	8,831.86	0.00
	$38,153.56	$4,033.80	$34,119.76	

(a) Lease payment as required by lease.
(b) Eight percent of the preceding balance of (d) except for 1/1/17; since this is an annuity due, no time has elapsed at the date of the first payment and therefore no interest has accrued.
(c) (a) minus (b).
(d) Preceding balance minus (c).
*Rounded by $0.02.

Parker computes straight-line expense and amortization on its right-of-use asset for each year of the lease, as presented in Illustration 21C-8.

ILLUSTRATION 21C-8
Lease Expense Schedule

	PARKER SHIPPING CO.			
	LEASE EXPENSE SCHEDULE			
Date	(A) Lease Expense (Straight-Line)	(B) Interest (8%) on Liability	(C) Amortization of ROU Asset (A − B)	(D) Carrying Value of ROU Asset (D − C)
12/31/16				$34,119.76
12/31/17	$ 9,538.39	$1,966.51	$ 7,571.88	26,547.88
12/31/18	9,538.39	1,360.76	8,177.63	18,370.25
12/31/19	9,538.39	706.53	8,831.86	9,538.39
12/31/20	9,538.39		9,538.39	0.00
	$38,153.56	$4,033.80	$34,119.76	

As indicated, the annual lease expense equals interest related to amortizing its lease liability plus amortization of the right-of-use asset. Parker decreases the right-of-use asset's book value each year by an amount (a plug) such that total annual lease expense is $9,538.39. The journal entries by Parker over the life of the lease are presented in Illustration 21C-9.

Parker Shipping (Lessee)

Recognize lease expense, record amortization (December 31, 2017):

Lease Expense	9,538.39	
Right-of-Use Asset		7,571.88
Lease Liability		1,966.51

Balance Sheet		**Income Statement**	
Noncurrent assets		Lease expense	$9,538.39
Right-of-use assets	$26,547.88		
Current liabilities			
Lease liability	$9,538.39		
Noncurrent liabilities			
Lease liability	17,009.49		

Record second lease payment (January 1, 2018):

Lease Liability	9,538.39	
Cash		9,538.39

Recognize lease expense, record amortization (December 31, 2018):

Lease Expense	9,538.39	
Right-of-Use Asset		8,177.63
Lease Liability		1,360.76

Balance Sheet		**Income Statement**	
Noncurrent assets		Lease expense	$9,538.39
Right-of-use assets	$18,370.25		
Current liabilities			
Lease liability	$9,538.39		
Noncurrent liabilities			
Lease liability	8,831.86		

Record third lease payment (January 1, 2019):

Lease Liability	9,538.39	
Cash		9,538.39

Recognize lease expense, record amortization (December 31, 2019):

Lease Expense	9,538.39	
Right-of-Use Asset		8,831.86
Lease Liability		706.53

Balance Sheet		**Income Statement**	
Noncurrent assets		Lease expense	$9,538.39
Right-of-use assets	$9,538.39		
Current liabilities			
Lease liability	$9,538.39		

Record lease payment (January 1, 2020):

Lease Liability	9,538.39	
Cash		9,538.39

Recognize lease expense, record amortization (December 31, 2020):

Lease Expense	9,538.39	
Right-of-Use Asset		9,538.39

After the entry for the final payment on December 31, 2020, the lease liability and right-of-use asset are fully amortized. The lease expense for the four years ($38,153.56) is comprised of amortization of the right of-use asset of $34,119.76 plus interest associated with the amortization of the lease liability of $4,033.80. Parker combines interest on the liability and amortization of the right-of-use asset to report lease expense on the income statement over the life of the lease.

Lessor Accounting—Operating Lease

As shown in the evaluation of the classification tests in Illustration 21C-6, Stoughton classifies the lease as an operating lease because none of the sales-type lease criteria are met. Stoughton's entries throughout the lease are presented in Illustration 21C-10.

ILLUSTRATION 21C-10
Lessor Entries for Operating Lease

Stoughton Trailers (Lessor)		
Lease payments (January 1, 2017, 2018, 2019, 2020):		
Cash	9,538.39	
Unearned Revenue		9,538.39
Recognize lease revenue, record depreciation (December 31, 2017, 2018, 2019, 2020):		
Unearned Revenue (leases)	9,538.39	
Lease Revenue		9,538.39
Depreciation Expense ($40,000.00 ÷ 6)	6,666.67	
Accumulated Depreciation—Equipment		6,666.67

Under the operating method, Stoughton (the lessor) continues to recognize the asset on its balance sheet and recognizes equal amounts of rental revenue (straight-line basis) in each period. It depreciates the leased asset generally on a straight-line basis over the asset's remaining economic life. In addition to the depreciation charge, Stoughton reports lease revenue separately from other revenues in its income statement or notes to its financial statements. A lessor should classify the leased equipment and accompanying accumulated depreciation separately from plant assets it owns as Equipment Leased to Others or Investment in Leased Property.

REVIEW AND PRACTICE

KEY TERMS REVIEW

bargain purchase option, 21-9

bargain renewal option, 21-9

capitalization of leases, 21-6

*direct financing lease, 21-39

executory costs, 21-27

failed sale, 21-36

finance lease, 21-7, 21-8

guaranteed residual value, 21-10

implicit interest rate, 21-11

incremental borrowing rate, 21-11

initial direct costs, 21-28

internal costs, 21-28

lease, 21-6

lease classification tests, 21-8

Lease Receivable, 21-15

lease term, 21-4

lease term test, 21-9

lessee, 21-3

lessor, 21-3

operating lease, 21-7, 21-8

residual value, 21-10

*sale-leaseback, 21-34

sales-type lease, 21-15

short-term lease, 21-29

unguaranteed residual value, 21-10

LEARNING OBJECTIVES REVIEW

1 Understand the environment related to leasing transactions. A lease is a contract, or part of a contract, that conveys the right to control the use of identified property, plant, or equipment (an identified asset) for a period of time in exchange for consideration. The advantages of lease transactions for lessees are (1) 100 percent financing, (2) protection against obsolescence, (3) flexibility, and (4) less costly financing. Lessors leasing benefits relate to (1) profitable interest margins, (2) stimulation of product sales, (3) tax benefits and efficient tax sharing, and (4) residual value profits. Lessees classify a lease as a finance lease if it meets one or more of the following tests: (1) the lease transfers ownership of the property to the lessee, (2) the lease contains an option to purchase the underlying asset that the lessee is reasonably certain to exercise, (3) the lease term is a major part (75%) of the remaining economic life of the underlying asset, (4) the present value of the lease payments equals or exceeds substantially all (90%) of the underlying asset's fair value, and (5) the lessor does not have an alternative use for the asset at the end of the lease. Lessors evaluate the same tests as lessees to determine the classification of a lease as sales-type or operating.

2 Explain the accounting for finance leases. For a finance/sales-type lease, the lessee records a right-of-use asset and related liability at the commencement of the lease. The lessee recognizes interest expense on the lease liability over the life of the lease using the effective-interest method and records amortization expense on the right-of-use asset. The lessor determines the lease payments, based on the rate of return—the implicit rate—needed to justify leasing the asset, taking into account the credit standing of the lessee, the length of the lease, and the status of the residual value (guaranteed versus unguaranteed). For a sales-type lease, the lessor accounts for the lease in a manner similar to the sale of an asset. At lease commencement, the lessor takes the asset off the books and records a receivable equal to the present value of the lease payments. Any dealer or manufacturer selling profit on the transfer of the leased asset is recognized in income at commencement of the lease. The lessor recognizes interest revenue on the lease receivable over the life of the lease using the effective-interest method.

3 Explain the accounting for operating leases. In an operating lease, a lessee obtains control of only **the use of the underlying asset but not ownership of the underlying asset itself.** Lessees and lessors classify and account for all leases that fail to meet any of the five classification tests as operating leases. Lessees account for operating leases using the straight-line, single-lease cost approach. Lease expense is recorded using the straight-line approach for operating leases. To achieve a single operating cost that is constant from period to period, companies continue to use the effective-interest method for amortizing the lease liability. However, instead of reporting interest expense, a lessee reports interest on the lease liability as part of Lease Expense. In addition, the lessee no longer reports amortization expense related to the right-of-use asset. Instead, it "plugs" in an amount that increases the Lease Expense account so that it is the same amount from period to period. This plugged amount then reduces the right-of-use asset, such that both the right-of-use asset and the lease liability are amortized to zero at the end of the lease. Under the operating method, lessors continue to recognize the asset on the balance sheet and record equal amounts of lease revenue (straight-line basis) in each period. It depreciates the leased asset generally on a straight-line basis.

4 Discuss the accounting and reporting for special features of lease arrangements. The features of lease arrangements that cause unique accounting problems are (1) residual values, (2) other lease adjustments (including initial direct costs), (3) bargain purchase options, (4) short-term leases (lessee), and (5) presentation, disclosure, and analysis.

The Effect of Residual Values, Guaranteed and Unguaranteed. In setting the lease payments, lessors work under the assumption that the residual value at the end of the lease term will be realized whether guaranteed or unguaranteed. This ensures that the lessor will recover the same net investment whether the residual value is guaranteed or unguaranteed. Whether the estimated residual value is guaranteed or unguaranteed is of both economic and accounting consequence to the lessee. The accounting consequence is that the lease payments, the basis for classification, include the guaranteed residual value but exclude the unguaranteed residual value. For measuring the lessee's lease liability and right-of-use asset, however, only the amount of the guaranteed residual value that is probable to be paid under the guarantee is included in the lease payments to be capitalized. In effect, the guaranteed residual value is an additional lease payment that the lessee will pay in property or cash, or both, at the end of the lease term. An unguaranteed residual value from the lessee's viewpoint is the same as no residual value in terms of its effect upon the lessee's method of computing the lease payments and the capitalization of the leased asset and the lease liability. See Illustration 21-28 for a summary.

Other Lease Adjustments. The lease liability is the starting point to determine the amount to record for the right-of-use asset. Companies adjust the measurement of the right-of-use asset as follows: (1) lease prepayments made by the lessee increase the right-of-use asset, (2) lease incentive payments made by the lessor to the lessee reduce the right-of-use asset, and (3) initial direct costs incurred by the lessee increase the right-of-use asset. Incremental costs of a lease that would not have been incurred had the lease not been executed are included in the cost of the right-of-use asset but should not be recorded as part of the lease liability. For operating leases, lessors defer initial direct costs and amortize them as expenses over the term of the lease. For sales-type leases, lessors generally expense initial direct costs at lease commencement. Lessor internal costs are not included in initial direct costs and are expensed as incurred.

Bargain Purchase Option. A bargain purchase option increases the present value of the lease payments by the present value of the option price for the lessee. In computing annual amortization of the right-of-use asset with this type of option, the lessee uses the economic life of the underlying asset.

Short-Term Leases. A short-term lease is a lease that, at the commencement date, has a lease term of 12 months or less. Rather than recording a right-of-use asset and lease liability, lessees may elect to forego recognition of a right-of-use asset and lease liability. If this election is taken, the lease payments are recognized in net income on a straight-line basis over the lease term. Variable lease payments for short-term leases should be recorded in the period in which the obligation for the payment is incurred.

Presentation, Disclosure, and Analysis. Presentation and disclosure by lessors and lessees of amounts related to leases vary depending on whether leases are classified as finance/sales-type or operating. See Illustrations 21-33 and 21-34 (presentation in the balance sheet and income statement) and Illustrations 21-35, 21-36, and 21-38 (disclosures in the notes to the financial statements) for summaries of presentation and disclosure requirements. Expanded recognition of lease assets and liabilities under the new lease accounting rules have the potential to result in significant impacts on analysis, based on information in the financial statements. A number of financial metrics used to measure the profitability and solvency of companies (return on assets and debt to equity ratios) will change, which could create challenges when performing financial analysis.

*5 Describe the lessee's accounting for sale-leaseback transactions. In a sale-leaseback arrangement, a company (the seller-lessee) transfers an asset to another company (the buyer-lessor) and then leases that asset back from the buyer-lessor. If the leaseback is classified as a finance/sales-type lease, the sale is not recognized (referred to as a failed sale) because the seller-lessee continues to control the asset—the transaction is accounted for as a financing arrangement. If the leaseback is classified as an operating lease, sale-leaseback accounting is appropriate. Under sale-leaseback accounting, gross profit on the sale is recognized and the leaseback is accounted for as an operating lease with recognition of a right-of-use asset, lease liability, and subsequent amortization, resulting in straight-line expense recognition. The buyer-lessor continues to recognize the asset on its balance sheet and recognizes equal amounts of lease revenue (straight-line basis) in each period. It depreciates the leased asset generally on a straight-line basis.

*6 Describe the lessor's accounting for a direct financing lease. In a direct financing lease, the lessee does not **obtain ownership control** of the asset, but the lessor **relinquishes control**. That is, the lessee controls use of the asset during the lease but will return the asset to the lessor at the end of the lease. However, the lessor will recover the value of the asset through lease payments **plus the third-party residual value guarantee**. In this situation, rather than following operating lease accounting: (1) the lessor derecognizes the underlying asset and recognizes a net investment in the lease (which consists of the lease receivable, unguaranteed residual asset, and deferred gross profit), and (2) the lessor gross profit is deferred and amortized into income over the lease term.

*7 Apply lessee and lessor accounting to finance and operating leases. Companies must understand and correctly apply the procedures for classifying and accounting for lease arrangements.

ENHANCED REVIEW AND PRACTICE

Go online for multiple-choice questions with solutions, review exercises with solutions, and a full glossary of all key terms.

PRACTICE PROBLEM

Morgan Bakeries is involved in four different lease situations. Each of these leases is non-cancelable, and in no case does Morgan receive title to the properties leased during or at the end of the lease term. All leases start on January 1, 2017, with the first rental due at the beginning of the year. For each lease, assume that the lessors have alternative use for the assets at the end of the lease unless ownership transfers to the lessee. Additional information is shown in the table on page 21-52.

	(a) Harmon, Inc.	(b) Arden's Oven Co.	(c) Mendota Truck Co.	(d) Appleland Computer
Type of property	Cabinets	Oven	Truck	Computer
Yearly rental	$6,000	$12,000	$5,189.31	$2,640.35
Lease term (years)	20	10	3	3
Estimated economic life	30	25	4	5
Purchase option	None	$75,000 at end of 10 years $4,000 at end of 15 years	None	$3,000 at end of 3 years, which approximates fair value
Renewal option	None	5-year renewal at $12,000 per year after 10 years, reasonably certain to be exercised if the purchase option is not	None	1 year at $1,500; no penalty for nonre-newal; standard renewal clause
Fair value at commencement of lease	$75,000	$120,000	$20,000	$10,000
Cost of asset to lessor	$60,000	$100,000	$15,000	$10,000
Residual value				
Guaranteed	–0–	–0–	$7,000 (the amount expected to be paid)	–0–
Unguaranteed	$35,000	–0–	–0–	$3,000
Incremental borrowing rate of lessee	8%	8%	8%	8%
Present value of rental payments				
Using incremental borrowing rate of lessee	$63,621.60	$112,191.84	$20,000	$7,618.51
Using implicit rate of lessor	Not known	Not known	Not known	Known by lessee (6%), $7,481.14
Estimated fair value at end of lease term	$35,000	$80,000 at end of 10 years $60,000 at end of 15 years	Not available	$3,000

Instructions

For each lease arrangement, determine the correct classification of the lease and prepare the journal entry at its commencement.

SOLUTION

(a) ANALYSIS OF THE HARMON, INC. LEASE:

1. **Transfer of title?** No.
2. **Bargain purchase option?** No.
3. **Economic life test (75% test):** The lease term is 20 years and the estimated economic life is 30 years. Thus, it **does not** meet the 75% test.
4. **Present value test (90% test):** No; the present value of the rental payments of $63,621,60 is less than 90 percent of the fair value of the underlying asset as shown below.

Fair value	$75,000		Rental payments	$ 6,000
Rate	× 90%		PV of annuity due for	
90% of fair value	$67,500		20 years at 8%	× 10.60360
			PV of rental payments	$63,621.60

Both Morgan and Harmon should account for this lease as an operating lease. They make the following January 1, 2017, entries.

Morgan Bakeries (Lessee)			Harmon, Inc. (Lessor)		
Right-of-Use Asset	63,621.60		Cash	6,000	
Lease Liability		63,621.60	Rent Revenue		6,000
Lease Liability	6,000.00				
Cash		6,000.00			

(b) ANALYSIS OF THE ARDEN'S OVEN CO. LEASE:

1. **Transfer of title?** No.

2. **Bargain purchase option?** The $75,000 option at the end of 10 years does not appear to be sufficiently lower than the expected fair value of $80,000 to make it reasonably assured that it will be exercised. However, given that the renewal option is reasonably certain to be exercised, the parties also consider the $4,000 purchase option at the end of 15 years. Since the fair value is expected to be $60,000 at the end of 15 years, the $4,000 option appears to be a bargain and test 2 (bargain purchase option) is therefore met. Note that both the guaranteed and the unguaranteed residual values are assigned zero values because the lessor does not expect to repossess the leased asset.

3. **Economic life test (75% test):** Given that the renewal option exists, the lease term is the initial lease period of 10 years plus the 5-year renewal option. Even though the lease term is now considered to be 15 years, the lease term test is still not met because 75 percent of the economic life of 25 years is 18.75 years.

4. **Present value test (90% test):**

Fair value	$120,000	Rental payments	$ 12,000
Rate	× 90%	PV of annuity due for	
90% of fair value	$108,000	15 years at 8%	× 9.24424
		PV of rental payments	$110,930.88

PV of bargain purchase option: = $4,000 × (PVF$_{15,8\%}$) = $4,000 × .31524 = $1,260.96

PV of rental payments	$110,930.88
PV of bargain purchase option	1,260.96
PV of lease payments	$112,191.84

The present value of the lease payments is greater than 90 percent of the fair value. Therefore, the lease does meet the 90% test.

Morgan should account for this as a finance lease, and Arden as a sales-type lease, because the lease meets both tests 2 and 4. The following entries are made on January 1, 2017.

Morgan Bakeries (Lessee)			Arden's Oven Co. (Lessor)		
Right-of Use Asset (oven)	112,191.84		Lease Receivable	120,000	
Lease Liability		112,191.84	Cost of Goods Sold	100,000	
Lease Liability	12,000.00		Inventory		100,000
Cash		12,000.00	Sales Revenue		120,000
			Cash	12,000	
			Lease Receivable		12,000

Morgan would amortize the right-of-use asset over its economic life of 25 years, given the bargain purchase option. The Lease Receivable amount of $120,000 recorded by Arden is different than the Lease Liability amount of $112,191.84 recorded by Morgan. The reason for this difference is that the implicit rate used by Arden is lower than the incremental borrowing rate of 8% used by Morgan.

(c) ANALYSIS OF THE MENDOTA TRUCK CO. LEASE:

1. **Transfer of title?** No.

2. **Bargain purchase option?** No.

3. **Economic life test (75% test):** The lease term is 3 years and the estimated economic life is 4 years. Thus, it **does** meet the 75% test (3 ÷ 4 = 75%).

4. **Present value test (90% test):**

Fair value	$20,000	Rental payments	$5,189.31
Rate	× 90%	PV of annuity due for	
90% of fair value	$18,000	3 years at 8%	× 2.78326
		PV of rental payments	$14,443.19*

*Adjusted for $0.01 due to rounding.

PV of guaranteed residual value = $7,000 × (PVF$_{3,8\%}$) = $7,000 × .79383 = $5,556.81

PV of rental payments	$14,443.19
PV of guaranteed residual value	5,556.81
PV of lease payments	$20,000.00

The present value of the lease payments is greater than 90 percent of the fair value. Therefore, the lease meets the 90% test.

The following entries are made on January 1, 2017.

Morgan Bakeries (Lessee)			Mendota Truck Co. (Lessor)		
Right-of-Use Asset (truck)	20.000.00		Lease Receivable	20,000	
Lease Liability		20.000.00	Cost of Goods Sold	15,000	
Lease Liability	5,189.31		Trucks		15,000
Cash		5,189.31	Sales Revenue		20,000
			Cash	5,189.31	
			Lease Receivable		5, 189.31

This is a sales-type lease for Mendota. Morgan amortizes the right-of-use asset over 3 years.

(d) ANALYSIS OF THE APPLELAND COMPUTER LEASE:

1. **Transfer of title?** No.
2. **Bargain purchase option?** No. The option to purchase at the end of 3 years at approximate fair value is clearly not a bargain.
3. **Economic life test (75% test):** The lease term is 3 years, and no bargain renewal period exists as it is simply a standard renewal clause which is not reasonably certain to be exercised. Therefore, the 75% test is not met (3 ÷ 5 = 60%).
4. **Recovery of investment test (90% test):**

Fair value	$10,000		Rental payments	$2,640.35
Rate	× 90%		PV of annuity-due factor for	
90% of fair value	$ 9,000		3 years at 6%	×2.83339
			PV of lease payments	
			using implicit borrowing rate	$7,481.14

The present value of the lease payments using the implicit borrowing rate is $7,481.14. Because the present value of the lease payments is lower than 90 percent of the fair value, the lease does **not** meet the present value test.

The entries made for an operating lease on January 1, 2017, are as follows.

Morgan Bakeries (Lessee)			Appleland Computer (Lessor)		
Right-of-Use Asset (truck)	7,481.14		Cash	2,640.35	
Lease Liability		7,481.14	Lease Revenue		2,640.35
Lease Liability	2,640.35				
Cash		2,640.35			

WileyPLUS | Brief Exercises, Exercises, Problems, Problem Solution Walkthrough Videos, and many more learning and assessment tools and resources are available for practice in WileyPLUS.

Note: All asterisked Questions, Exercises, and Problems relate to material in the appendices to the chapter.

QUESTIONS

1. What are the major lessor groups in the United States? What advantage does a captive leasing subsidiary have in a leasing arrangement?

2. Bradley Co. is expanding its operations and is in the process of selecting the method of financing this program.

After some investigation, the company determines that it may (1) issue bonds and with the proceeds purchase the needed assets, or (2) lease the assets on a long-term basis. Without knowing the comparative costs involved, answer these questions:

(a) What are the possible advantages of leasing the assets instead of owning them?

(b) What are the possible disadvantages of leasing the assets instead of owning them?

(c) How will the balance sheet be different if Bradley Co. leases the assets rather than purchasing them?

3. What are the major advantages to a lessor for becoming involved in a leasing arrangement?

4. From a lessee perspective, distinguish between a finance lease and an operating lease.

5. Identify the lease classification tests and how they are applied.

6. Morgan Handley and Tricia Holbrook are discussing the new leasing standard. Morgan believes the standard requires that the lessee use the implicit rate of the lessor in computing the present value of its lease liability. Tricia is not sure if Morgan is correct. Explain the discount rate that the lessee should use to compute its lease liability.

7. Explain which of following would result in the lessee classifying the lease as a finance lease.

(a) The lease is for a major part of the economic life of the asset.

(b) The lease term is for 12 months or less.

(c) The lease transfers ownership of the asset at the end of the lease.

8. Paul Singer indicated that "all leases must now be capitalized on the balance sheet." Is this statement correct? Explain.

9. Describe the following terms: (a) residual value, (b) guaranteed residual value, and (c) initial direct costs.

10. Explain the following concepts: (a) bargain purchase option and (b) bargain renewal option.

11. What payments are included in the lease liability?

12. Wonda Stone read somewhere that a residual value guarantee is used for computing the present value of lease payments for lease classification purposes but is treated differently when measuring its lease liability. Is Wonda correct in her interpretation? Explain.

13. Identify the amounts included in the measurement of the right-of-use asset.

14. Harcourt Company enters into a lease agreement with Brunsell Inc. to lease office space for a term of 72 months. Lease payments during the first year are $5,000 per month. Each year thereafter, the lease payments increase by an amount equivalent to the percentage increase in the Consumer Price Index (CPI). For example, if the CPI increases 2% in the second year, the monthly payment increases to $5,100. In the second year, the CPI increases by 3%. What are the lease payment amounts used to record this lease in the second year?

15. Describe the accounting procedures involved in applying the operating lease method by a lessee.

16. Describe the accounting procedures involved in applying the finance lease method by a lessee.

17. Explain the difference in lessee income statement and balance sheet presentation for a finance versus an operating lease.

18. Dr. Alice Foyle (lessee) has a non-cancelable, 20-year lease with Brownback Realty Inc. (lessor) for the use of a medical building. Taxes, insurance, and maintenance are paid by the lessee in addition to the fixed annual payments, of which the present value is equal to the fair value of the leased property. At the end of the lease period, title becomes the lessee's at a nominal price. Considering the terms of this lease, comment on the nature of the lease transaction and the accounting treatment that should be accorded it by the lessee.

19. Identify the lease classifications for lessors and the criteria that must be met for each classification. What is the relevance of revenue recognition criteria for lessor accounting for leases?

20. What is the difference between a lease receivable and a net investment in the lease?

21. Explain the accounting involved in applying the operating lease method by a lessor.

22. Explain the difference in lessor income statement presentation for a sales-type versus operating lease.

23. Walker Company is a manufacturer and lessor of computer equipment. What should be the nature of its lease arrangements with lessees if the company wishes to account for its lease transactions as sales-type leases?

24. Metheny Corporation's lease arrangements qualify as sales-type leases at the time of entering into the transactions. How should the corporation recognize sales revenue and cost of goods sold in these situations?

25. Packer Company (the lessor) concludes that its lease meets one of the tests to be classified as a sales-type lease. However, collection of lease payments is not probable. In this case, how should Packer account for any lease payments received?

26. The residual value is the estimated fair value of the leased property at the end of the lease term.

(a) Of what significance is (1) an unguaranteed and (2) a guaranteed residual value in the lessee's accounting for a finance lease transaction?

(b) Distinguish between lease payments used to determine lease classification compared to lease payments for measuring the lease liability.

27. Of what significance is (a) an unguaranteed and (b) a guaranteed residual value in the lessor's accounting for a sales-type lease transaction?

28. Describe the effect on the lessee of a "bargain purchase option" on accounting for a finance lease transaction.

29. What are "initial direct costs" and how are they accounted for by lessees and lessors?

30. What is a short-term lease? Describe lessee accounting for a short-term lease.

31. What disclosures should be made by lessees and lessors related to future lease payments?

*32. What is the nature of a "sale-leaseback" transaction?

*33. Sanchez Company (seller-lessee) enters into a sale-leaseback to sell its corporate headquarters for $18 million to Harper Bank. The carrying value of the headquarters at the date of sale is $14 million. Sanchez then leases back the headquarters in exchange for $180,000 per year in rental payments. The leaseback is considered an operating lease. How should Sanchez account for this sale?

*34. Explain the distinction between a direct financing lease and a sales-type lease for a lessor.

*35. Explain the differences in revenue recognition for the lessor in a sales-type lease, a direct financing lease, and an operating lease.

*36. Describe the accounting procedures involved in applying the direct financing method by a lessor.

BRIEF EXERCISES

BE21-1 (LO2) Callaway Golf Co. leases telecommunications equipment from Photon Company. Assume the following data for equipment leased from Photon Company. The lease term is 5 years and requires equal rental payments of $31,000 at the beginning of each year. The equipment has a fair value at the commencement of the lease of $150,000, an estimated useful life of 8 years, and a guaranteed residual value at the end of the lease of $15,500. Photon set the annual rental to earn a rate of return of 6%, and this fact is known to Callaway. The lease does not transfer title or contain a bargain purchase option, and is not a specialized asset. How should Callaway classify this lease?

BE21-2 (LO2) Jelly Co. processes jam and sells it to the public. Jelly leases equipment used in its production processes from Squishy, Inc. This year, Jelly leases a new piece of equipment from Squishy. The lease term is 5 years and requires equal rental payments of $15,000 at the beginning of each year. In addition, there is a renewal option to allow Jelly to keep the equipment one extra year for a payment at the end of the fifth year of $10,000 (which Jelly is reasonably certain it will exercise). The equipment has a fair value at the commencement of the lease of $76,024 and an estimated useful life of 7 years. Squishy set the annual rental to earn a rate of return of 5%, and this fact is known to Jelly. The lease does not transfer title, does not contain a bargain purchase option, and the equipment is not of a specialized nature. How should Jelly classify this lease?

BE21-3 (LO2) Samson Company leases a building and land. The lease term is 6 years and the annual fixed payments are $800,000. The lease arrangement gives Samson the right to purchase the building and land for $11,000,000 at the end of the lease. Based on an economic analysis of the lease at the commencement date, Samson is reasonably certain that the fair value of the leased assets at the end of lease term will be much higher than $11,000,000. What are the total lease payments in this lease arrangement?

BE21-4 (LO2,4) Fieger Company leases equipment for 8 years with an annual rental of $2,000 per year or $16,000 in total. General Leasing (the lessor) agrees to provide Fieger with $300 for the first 2 years of the lease to defray needed repairs to the equipment. Determine the lease payments that Fieger will pay for the first 3 years of the lease agreement.

BE21-5 (LO1) Sanders Fashion Company enters into a lease arrangement with Highpoint Leasing for 5 years. Sanders agrees to pay 4% of its net sales as a variable lease payment. Sanders does not pay any fixed payments. Sanders is a highly successful company that has achieved over $1,000,000 in net sales over the last 7 years. Both Sanders and Highpoint forecast that net sales will be a much greater amount than $1,000,000 in subsequent years. As a result, it is highly certain that Sanders will make payments of at least $40,000 ($1,000,000 × 4%) each year. What is the lease payment amount Sanders should use to record its right-of-use asset?

BE21-6 (LO2) Waterworld Company leased equipment from Costner Company, beginning on December 31, 2016. The lease term is 4 years and requires equal rental payments of $41,933 at the beginning of each year of the lease, starting on the commencement date (December 31, 2016). The equipment has a fair value at the commencement date of the lease of $150,001, an estimated useful life of 4 years, and no estimated residual value. The appropriate interest rate is 8%. Prepare Waterworld's 2016 and 2017 journal entries, assuming Waterworld depreciates similar equipment it owns on a straight-line basis.

BE21-7 (LO2) Rick Kleckner Corporation recorded a right-of-use asset for $300,000 as a result of a finance lease on December 31, 2016. Kleckner's incremental borrowing rate is 8%, and the implicit rate of the lessor was not known at the commencement of the lease. Kleckner made the first lease payment of $48,337 on December 31, 2016. The lease requires eight annual payments. The equipment has a useful life of 8 years with no residual value. Prepare Kleckner's December 31, 2017, entries.

BE21-8 (LO2,4) Cardinal Company is negotiating to lease a piece of equipment to MTBA, Inc. MTBA requests that the lease be for 9 years. The equipment has a useful life of 10 years. Cardinal wants a guarantee that the residual value of the equipment at the end of the lease is at least $5,000. MTBA agrees to guarantee a residual value of this amount though it expects the residual value of the equipment to be only $2,500 at the end of the lease term. If the fair value of the equipment at lease commencement is $70,000, what would be the amount of the annual rental payments Cardinal demands of MTBA, assuming each payment will be made at the beginning of each year and Cardinal wishes to earn a rate of return on the lease of 8%?

BE21-9 (LO1,4) Mequon Inc. wishes to lease machinery to Thiensville Company. Thiensville wants the machinery for 4 years, although it has a useful life of 10 years. The machinery has a fair value at the commencement of the lease of $47,000, and Mequon expects the machinery to have a residual value at the end of the lease term of $30,000. However, Thiensville does not guarantee any part of the residual value. Thiensville does expect that the residual value will be $45,000 instead of $30,000. What would be the amount of the annual rental payments Mequon demands of Thiensville, assuming each payment will be made at the end of each year and Mequon wishes to earn a rate of return on the lease of 6%?

BE21-10 (LO2) Assume that IBM leased equipment that was carried at a cost of $120,000 to Swander Company. The term of the lease is 6 years beginning December 31, 2016, with equal rental payments of $30,043.80 beginning December 31, 2016. The fair value of the equipment at commencement of the lease is $150,001. The equipment has a useful life of 6 years with no salvage value. The lease has an implicit interest rate of 8%, no bargain purchase option, and no transfer of title. Collectibility of lease payments for IBM is probable. Prepare Swander's December 31, 2016, journal entries at commencement of the lease.

BE21-11 (LO2) Use the information for IBM from BE21-10. Assume the sales-type lease was recorded at a present value of $150,000. Prepare IBM's December 31, 2017, entry to record the lease transaction with Swander Company.

BE21-12 (LO2) Geiberger Corporation manufactures drones. On December 31, 2016, it leased to Althaus Company a drone that had cost $120,000 to manufacture. The lease agreement covers the 5-year useful life of the drone and requires five equal annual rentals of $40,800 payable each December 31, beginning December 31, 2016. An interest rate of 8% is implicit in the lease agreement. Collectibility of the rentals is probable. Prepare Geiberger's December 31, 2016, journal entries.

BE21-13 (LO2) Use the information for Geiberger Corporation from BE21-12, except assume the collectibility of the rentals is not probable. Prepare any journal entries for Geiberger on December 31, 2016.

BE21-14 (LO2) Kubby Company specializes in leasing large storage units to other businesses. Kubby entered a contract to lease a storage unit to Riskey, Inc. for 4 years when that particular storage unit had a remaining useful life of 5 years. The fair value of the unit was $10,000 at the commencement of the lease on January 1, 2017. The present value of the five equal rental payments of $2,507 at the start of each year, plus the present value of a guaranteed residual value of $1,000, equals the fair value of $10,000, Kubby's implicit rate of return on the lease of 6%. The following is a correct, complete amortization schedule created by Kubby.

Date	Lease Payment	Interest (6%) on Outstanding Lease Receivable	Reduction of Lease Receivable	Balance of Lease Receivable
1/1/17				$10,000
1/1/17	$ 2,507		$ 2,507	7,493
1/1/18	2,507	$ 450	2,057	5,436
1/1/19	2,507	326	2,181	3,255
1/1/20	2,507	195	2,312	943
12/31/20	1,000	57	943	0
	$11,028	$1,028	$10,000	

Given the above schedule, make the appropriate entries at December 31, 2020, to record the accrual of interest and the return of the storage unit to Kubby (assuming the unit is returned on December 31, 2020, at the expected and guaranteed residual value of $1,000).

BE21-15 (LO3) LeBron James (LBJ) Corporation agrees on January 1, 2017, to lease equipment from Cavaliers, Inc. for 3 years. The lease calls for annual lease payments of $23,000 at the beginning of each year. The lease does not transfer ownership, nor does it contain a bargain purchase option, and is not a specialized asset. In addition, the useful life of the equipment is 10 years, and the present value of the lease payments is less than 90% of the fair value of the equipment. Prepare LBJ's journal entries on January 1, 2017 (commencement of the operating lease), and on December 31, 2017. Assume the implicit rate used by the lessor is unknown, and LBJ's incremental borrowing rate is 6%.

BE21-16 (LO3) Kingston Corporation leases equipment from Falls Company on January 1, 2017. The lease agreement does not transfer ownership, contain a bargain purchase option, and is not a specialized asset. It covers 3 years of the equipment's 8-year useful life, and the present value of the lease payments is less than 90% of the fair value of the asset leased. Prepare Kingston's journal entries on January 1, 2017, and December 31, 2017. Assume the annual lease payment is $35,000 at the beginning of each year, and Kingston's incremental borrowing rate is 6%, which is the same as the lessor's implicit rate.

BE21-17 (LO3) Use the information for Kingston Corporation from BE21-16. Prepare all the necessary journal entries for Falls Company (the lessor) for 2017, assuming the equipment is carried at a cost of $200,000.

BE21-18 (LO3) Rodgers Corporation agrees on January 1, 2017, to lease equipment from Packers, Inc. for 3 years. The lease calls for annual lease payments of $12,000 at the beginning of each year. The lease does not transfer ownership, contain a bargain purchase option, and is not a specialized asset. In addition, the economic life of the equipment is 10 years, and the present value of the lease payments is less than 90% of the fair value of the equipment. Prepare Rodgers' journal entries on January 1, 2017 (commencement of the operating lease), and on December 31, 2017. Assume the implicit rate used by the lessor is 8%, and this is known to Rodgers.

BE21-19 (LO3) Use the information for Rodgers Corporation and Packers, Inc. from BE21-18. Assume that for Packers, Inc., the lessor, the collectibility of the lease payments is probable, and the fair value and cost of the equipment is $60,000. Prepare Packers' 2017 journal entries, assuming the company uses straight-line depreciation and no salvage value.

BE21-20 (LO4) On December 31, 2016, Escapee Company leased machinery from Terminator Corporation for an agreed-upon lease term of 3 years. Escapee agreed to make annual lease payments of $17,000, beginning on December 31, 2016. The expected residual value of the machinery at the end of the lease term is $9,000, though Escapee does not guarantee any residual value to Terminator. What amount will Escapee record as its lease liability on December 31, 2016, if its incremental borrowing rate is 6% and the implicit rate of the lease is unknown?

BE21-21 (LO4) Use the information for Escapee Company from BE21-20. Assume the same facts, except Escapee guarantees a residual value of $9,000 at the end of the lease term, which equals the expected residual value of the machinery. (a) Does this change your answer from BE21-20? (b) What if the expected residual value at the end of the lease term is $5,000 and Escapee guarantees a residual of $9,000?

BE21-22 (LO4) Indiana Jones Corporation enters into a 6-year lease of equipment on December 31, 2016, which requires six annual payments of $40,000 each, beginning December 31, 2016. In addition, Indiana Jones guarantees the lessor a residual value of $20,000 at the end of the lease. However, Indiana Jones believes it is probable that the expected residual value at the end of the lease term will be $10,000. The equipment has a useful life of 6 years. Prepare Indiana Jones' December 31, 2016, journal entries, assuming the implicit rate of the lease is 6% and this is known to Indiana Jones.

BE21-23 (LO4) Use the information for Indiana Jones Corporation from BE21-22. Assume that for Lost Ark Company, the lessor, collectibility of lease payments is probable and the carrying amount of the equipment is $180,000. Prepare Lost Ark's 2016 and 2017 journal entries.

BE21-24 (LO4) Forrest, Inc. has entered an agreement to lease an old warehouse with a useful life of 5 years and a fair value of $20,000 from United Corporation. The agreement stipulates the following.

* Rental payments of $4,638 are to be made at the start of each year of the 5-year lease. No residual value is expected at the end of the lease.

* Forrest must reimburse United each year for any real estate taxes incurred for the year. Last year, the cost of real estate taxes was $700, though these costs vary from year to year.

* Forrest must make a payment of $500 with the rental payment each period to cover the insurance United has on the warehouse.

* Forrest paid legal fees of $1,000 in executing the lease.

Assuming Forrest's incremental borrowing rate is 8% and the rate implicit in the lease is unknown, prepare the journal entry to record the initial lease liability and right-of-use asset for Forrest.

BE21-25 (LO4) Bucky Corporation entered into an operating lease agreement to lease equipment from Badger, Inc. on January 1, 2017. The lease calls for annual lease payments of $30,000, beginning on January 1, for each of the 3 years of the lease. In addition, Badger will pay Bucky $5,000 as a cash incentive for entering the lease by January 1, 2017. In relation to the lease agreement, Bucky incurred the following costs.

Salaries of employees involved in the investigation of the lease	$2,000
Lease document preparation costs incurred after execution of the lease	500

Bucky's incremental borrowing rate is 8%. If the value of the lease liability is $83,498, what amount will Bucky record as the value of the right-of-use asset on January 1, 2017, at commencement of the operating lease?

BE21-26 (LO4) Homestead Corporation entered into an operating lease to lease equipment from Highlander, Inc. on January 1, 2017. The lease calls for annual lease payments of $10,000, beginning on December 31, for each of the 5 years of the lease. In addition, Highlander, Inc. will pay Homestead Corporation $2,000 as a cash incentive for entering the lease by December 31. In relation to the lease agreement, Homestead incurred the following costs.

Commissions for selling agents	$ 900
Internal engineering costs	500
Legal fees resulting from the execution of the lease	3,000

Homestead's incremental borrowing rate is 6%. If the value of the lease liability is $44,651, what amount will Homestead record as the value of the right-of-use asset on January 1, 2017, at commencement of the operating lease?

BE21-27 (LO4) Debbink Co. leased machinery from Young, Inc. on January 1, 2017. The lease term was for 8 years, with equal annual rental payments of $5,300 at the beginning of each year. In addition, the lease provides an option to purchase the machinery at the end of the lease term for $2,000, which Debbink is reasonably certain it will exercise as it believes the fair value of the machinery will be at least $6,000. The machinery has a useful life of 10 years and a fair value of $36,000. The implicit rate of the lease is not known to Debbink. Debbink's incremental borrowing rate is 8%. Prepare Debbink's 2017 journal entries.

BE21-28 (LO4) Brent Corporation owns equipment that cost $80,000 and has a useful life of 8 years with no salvage value. On January 1, 2017, Brent leases the equipment to Havaci Inc. for one year for one rental payment of $15,000 on January 1. Assuming Havaci (lessee) elects to use the short-term lease exception, prepare Havaci's 2017 journal entries.

*__BE21-29__ (LO5) On January 1, 2017, Irwin Animation sold a truck to Peete Finance for $35,000 and immediately leased it back. The truck was carried on Irwin's books at $28,000. The term of the lease is 3 years, there is no bargain purchase option, and title does not transfer to Irwin at lease-end. The lease requires three equal rental payments of $8,696 at the end of each year (first payment on January 1, 2018). The appropriate rate of interest is 6%, the truck has a useful life of 5 years, and the residual value at the end of the lease term is expected to be $14,000, none of which is guaranteed. Prepare Irwin's 2017 journal entries.

*__BE21-30__ (LO5) Assume the same facts as BE21-29, except the lease term is now 5 years and the five annual rental payments are $8,309, with no expected residual value at the end of the lease term. Prepare Irwin's 2017 journal entries assuming these new facts.

*__BE21-31__ (LO6) Bulls, Inc. leases a piece of equipment to Bucks Company on January 1, 2017. The contract stipulates a lease term of 5 years, with equal annual rental payments of $4,523 at the end of each year. Ownership does not transfer at the end of the lease term, there is no bargain purchase option, and the asset is not of a specialized nature. The asset has a fair value of $30,000, a book value of $27,000, and a useful life of 8 years. At the end of the lease term, Bulls expects the residual value of the asset to be $12,000, and this amount is guaranteed by a third party. Assuming Bulls wants to earn a 4% return on the lease and collectibility of the lease payments is probable, record its journal entry at the commencement of the lease on January 1, 2017.

*__BE21-32__ (LO6) Use the information for Bulls, Inc. from BE21-31. Assume that the lease receivable is $30,000, deferred gross profit is $3,000, and the rate of return to amortize the net lease receivable to zero is 7.11%. Prepare Bulls' journal entry at the end of the first year of the lease to record the receipt of the first lease payment.

EXERCISES

__E21-1__ (LO1,4) (Lessee Entries; Finance Lease with No Residual Value) DU Journeys enters into an agreement with Traveler Inc. to lease a car on December 31, 2016. The following information relates to this agreement.

1. The term of the non-cancelable lease is 3 years with no renewal or bargain purchase option. The remaining economic life of the car is 3 years, and it is expected to have no residual value at the end of the lease term.
2. The fair value of the car was $15,000 at commencement of the lease.
3. Annual payments are required to be made on December 31 at the end of each year of the lease, beginning December 31, 2017. The first payment is to be of an amount of $5,552.82, with each payment increasing by a constant rate of 5% from the previous payment (i.e., the second payment will be $5,830.46 and the third and final payment will be $6,121.98).
4. DU Journeys' incremental borrowing rate is 8%. The rate implicit in the lease is unknown.
5. DU Journeys uses straight-line depreciation for all similar cars.

Instructions

(a) Prepare DU Journeys' journal entries for 2016, 2017, and 2018.
(b) Assume, instead of a constant rate of increase, the annual lease payments will increase according to the Consumer Price Index (CPI). At its current level, the CPI stipulates that the first rental payment should be $5,820. What would be the impact on the journal entries made by DU Journeys at commencement of the lease, as well as for subsequent years?

__E21-2__ (LO2,4) (Lessee Entries; Finance Lease with Unguaranteed Residual Value) On December 31, 2016, Burke Corporation signed a 5-year, non-cancelable lease for a machine. The terms of the lease called for Burke to make annual payments of $8,668 at the beginning of each year, starting December 31, 2016. The machine has an estimated useful life of 6 years and a $5,000 unguaranteed residual value. The machine reverts back to the lessor at the end of the lease term. Burke uses the straight-line method of depreciation for all of its plant assets. Burke's incremental borrowing rate is 5%, and the lessor's implicit rate is unknown.

Instructions

(a) What type of lease is this? Explain.
(b) Compute the present value of the lease payments.
(c) Prepare all necessary journal entries for Burke for this lease through December 31, 2017.

__E21-3__ (LO2,4) (Lessee Computations and Entries; Finance Lease with Guaranteed Residual Value) Delaney Company leases an automobile with a fair value of $10,000 from Simon Motors, Inc., on the following terms.

1. Non-cancelable term of 50 months.
2. Rental of $200 per month (at the beginning of each month). (The present value at 0.5% per month is $8,873.)
3. Delaney guarantees a residual value of $1,180 (the present value at 0.5% per month is $920). Delaney expects the probable residual value to be $1,180 at the end of the lease term.
4. Estimated economic life of the automobile is 60 months.
5. Delaney's incremental borrowing rate is 6% a year (0.5% a month). Simon's implicit rate is unknown.

Instructions

(a) What is the nature of this lease to Delaney?

(b) What is the present value of the lease payments to determine the lease liability?

(c) Based on the original fact pattern, record the lease on Delaney's books at the date of commencement.

(d) Record the first month's lease payment (at commencement of the lease).

(e) Record the second month's lease payment.

(f) Record the first month's amortization on Delaney's books (assume straight-line).

(g) Suppose that instead of $1,180, Delaney expects the residual value to be only $500 (the guaranteed amount is still $1,180). How does the calculation of the present value of the lease payments change from part (b)?

E21-4 (LO2,4) EXCEL (Lessee Entries; Finance Lease and Unguaranteed Residual Value) Assume that on December 31, 2016, Kimberly-Clark Corp. signs a 10-year, non-cancelable lease agreement to lease a storage building from Sheffield Storage Company. The following information pertains to this lease agreement.

1. The agreement requires equal rental payments of $71,830 beginning on December 31, 2016.

2. The fair value of the building on December 31, 2016, is $525,176.

3. The building has an estimated economic life of 12 years, a guaranteed residual value of $10,000, and an expected residual value of $7,000. Kimberly-Clark depreciates similar buildings on the straight-line method.

4. The lease is nonrenewable. At the termination of the lease, the building reverts to the lessor.

5. Kimberly-Clark's incremental borrowing rate is 8% per year. The lessor's implicit rate is not known by Kimberly-Clark.

Instructions

(a) Prepare the journal entries on the lessee's books to reflect the signing of the lease agreement and to record the payments and expenses related to this lease for the years 2016, 2017, and 2018. Kimberly-Clark's fiscal year-end is December 31.

(b) Suppose the same facts as above, except that Kimberly-Clark incurred legal fees resulting from the execution of the lease of $5,000, and received a lease incentive from Sheffield to enter the lease of $1,000. How would the initial measurement of the lease liability and right-of-use asset be affected under this situation?

(c) Suppose that in addition to the $71,830 annual rental payments, Kimberly-Clark is also required to pay $5,000 for insurance costs each year on the building directly to the lessor, Sheffield Storage. How would this executory cost affect the initial measurement of the lease liability and right-of-use asset?

(d) Return to the original facts in the problem. Now suppose that, at the end of the lease term, Kimberly-Clark took good care of the asset and Sheffield agrees that the fair value of the asset is actually $10,000. Record the entry for Kimberly-Clark at the end of the lease to return control of the storage building to Sheffield (assuming the accrual of interest on the lease liability has already been made).

E21-5 (LO2,4) (Computation of Rental; Journal Entries for Lessor) Morgan Leasing Company signs an agreement on January 1, 2017, to lease equipment to Cole Company. The following information relates to this agreement.

1. The term of the non-cancelable lease is 6 years with no renewal option. The equipment has an estimated economic life of 6 years.

2. The cost of the asset to the lessor is $245,000. The fair value of the asset at January 1, 2017, is $245,000.

3. The asset will revert to the lessor at the end of the lease term, at which time the asset is expected to have a residual value of $24,335, none of which is guaranteed.

4. The agreement requires equal annual rental payments, beginning on January 1, 2017.

5. Collectibility of the lease payments by Morgan is probable.

Instructions

(Round all numbers to the nearest cent.)

(a) Assuming the lessor desires an 8% rate of return on its investment, calculate the amount of the annual rental payment required. (Round to the nearest dollar.)

(b) Prepare an amortization schedule that is suitable for the lessor for the lease term.

(c) Prepare all of the journal entries for the lessor for 2017 and 2018 to record the lease agreement, the receipt of lease payments, and the recognition of revenue. Assume the lessor's annual accounting period ends on December 31, and it does not use reversing entries.

E21-6 (LO2,4) (Lessor Entries; Sales-Type Lease with Option to Purchase) Castle Leasing Company signs a lease agreement on January 1, 2017, to lease electronic equipment to Jan Way Company. The term of the non-cancelable lease is 2 years, and payments are required at the end of each year. The following information relates to this agreement.

1. Jan Way has the option to purchase the equipment for $16,000 upon termination of the lease. It is not reasonably certain that Jan Way will exercise this option.

2. The equipment has a cost of $120,000 and fair value of $160,000 to Castle Leasing. The useful economic life is 2 years, with a residual value of $16,000.

3. Castle Leasing desires to earn a return of 5% on its investment.

4. Collectibility of the payments by Castle Leasing is probable.

Instructions

(a) Prepare the journal entries on the books of Castle Leasing to reflect the payments received under the lease and to recognize income for the years 2017 and 2018.

(b) Assuming that Jan Way exercises its option to purchase the equipment on December 31, 2018, prepare the journal entry to record the sale on Castle Leasing's books.

E21-7 (LO2,4) (Type of Lease; Amortization Schedule) Macinski Leasing Company leases a new machine to Sharrer Corporation. The machine has a cost of $70,000 and fair value of $95,000. Under the 3-year, non-cancelable contract, Sharrer will receive title to the machine at the end of the lease. The machine has a 3-year useful life and no residual value. The lease was signed on January 1, 2017. Macinski expects to earn an 8% return on its investment, and this implicit rate is known by Sharrer. The annual rentals are payable on each December 31, beginning December 31, 2017.

Instructions

(a) Discuss the nature of the lease arrangement and the accounting method that each party to the lease should apply.

(b) Prepare an amortization schedule that would be suitable for both the lessor and the lessee and that covers all the years involved.

(c) Prepare the journal entry at commencement of the lease for Macinski.

(d) Prepare the journal entry at commencement of the lease for Sharrer.

(e) Prepare the journal entry at commencement of the lease for Sharrer, assuming (1) Sharrer does not know Macinski's implicit rate (Sharrer's incremental borrowing rate is 9%), and (2) Sharrer incurs initial directs costs of $10,000.

E21-8 (LO2,4) EXCEL (Lessor Entries; Sales-Type Lease) Crosley Company, a machinery dealer, leased a machine to Dexter Corporation on January 1, 2017. The lease is for an 8-year period and requires equal annual payments of $35,004 at the beginning of each year. The first payment is received on January 1, 2017. Crosley had purchased the machine during 2016 for $160,000. Collectibility of lease payments by Crosley is probable. Crosley set the annual rental to ensure a 6% rate of return. The machine has an economic life of 10 years with no residual value and reverts to Crosley at the termination of the lease.

Instructions

(a) Compute the amount of the lease receivable.

(b) Prepare all necessary journal entries for Crosley for 2017.

(c) Suppose the collectibility of the lease payments was not probable for Crosley. Prepare all necessary journal entries for the company in 2017.

(d) Suppose at the end of the lease term, Crosley receives the asset and determines that it actually has a fair value of $1,000 instead of the anticipated residual value of $0. Record the entry to recognize the receipt of the asset for Crosley at the end of the lease term.

E21-9 (LO2,4) (Lessee Entries; Initial Direct Costs) Use the information for Crosley Company in E21-8. Assume that Dexter Corporation does not know the rate implicit in the lease used by Crosley, and Dexter's incremental borrowing rate is 8%. In addition, assume that Dexter incurs initial direct costs of $15,000.

Instructions

(a) Compute the amount of the lease liability and right-of-use asset for Dexter.

(b) Prepare all necessary journal entries for Dexter for 2017.

E21-10 (LO2,4) (Lessee Entries with Bargain Purchase Option) The following facts pertain to a non-cancelable lease agreement between Mooney Leasing Company and Rode Company, a lessee.

Commencement date	May 1, 2017
Annual lease payment due at the beginning of each year, beginning with May 1, 2017	$20,471.94
Bargain purchase option price at end of lease term	$ 4,000.00
Lease term	5 years
Economic life of leased equipment	10 years
Lessor's cost	$65,000.00
Fair value of asset at May 1, 2017	$91,000.00
Lessor's implicit rate	8%
Lessee's incremental borrowing rate	8%
The collectibility of the lease payments by Mooney is probable.	

Instructions

(Round all numbers to the nearest cent.)

(a) Discuss the nature of this lease to Rode.

(b) Discuss the nature of this lease to Mooney.

(c) Prepare a lease amortization schedule for Rode for the 5-year lease term.

(d) Prepare the journal entries on the lessee's books to reflect the signing of the lease agreement and to record the payments and expenses related to this lease for the years 2017 and 2018. Rode's annual accounting period ends on December 31. Reversing entries are used by Rode.

E21-11 (LO2,4) (Lessor Entries with Bargain Purchase Option) A lease agreement between Mooney Leasing Company and Rode Company is described in E21-10.

Instructions

Refer to the data in E21-10 and do the following for the lessor. (Round all numbers to the nearest cent.)

(a) Compute the amount of the lease receivable at commencement of the lease.

(b) Prepare a lease amortization schedule for Mooney for the 5-year lease term.

(c) Prepare the journal entries to reflect the signing of the lease agreement and to record the receipts and income related to this lease for the years 2017 and 2018. The lessor's accounting period ends on December 31. Reversing entries are not used by Mooney.

(d) Suppose the collectibility of the lease payments was not probable for Mooney. Prepare all necessary journal entries for the company in 2017.

E21-12 (LO2,4) (Lessee-Lessor Entries; Sales-Type Lease with Bargain Purchase Option) On January 1, 2017, Bensen Company leased equipment to Flynn Corporation. The following information pertains to this lease.

1. The term of the non-cancelable lease is 6 years. At the end of the lease term, Flynn has the option to purchase the equipment for $1,000, while the expected residual value at the end of the lease is $5,000.
2. Equal rental payments are due on January 1 of each year, beginning in 2017.
3. The fair value of the equipment on January 1, 2017, is $150,000, and its cost is $120,000.
4. The equipment has an economic life of 8 years. Flynn depreciates all of its equipment on a straight-line basis.
5. Bensen set the annual rental to ensure a 5% rate of return. Flynn's incremental borrowing rate is 6%, and the implicit rate of the lessor is unknown.
6. Collectibility of lease payments by the lessor is probable.

Instructions

(Both the lessor and the lessee's accounting periods end on December 31.)

(a) Discuss the nature of this lease to Bensen and Flynn.

(b) Calculate the amount of the annual rental payment.

(c) Prepare all the necessary journal entries for Bensen for 2017.

(d) Suppose the collectibility of the lease payments was not probable for Bensen. Prepare all necessary journal entries for the company in 2017.

(e) Prepare all the necessary journal entries for Flynn for 2017.

(f) Discuss the effect on the journal entry for Flynn at lease commencement, assuming initial direct costs of $2,000 are incurred by Flynn to negotiate the lease.

E21-13 (LO2,4) (Lessee-Lessor Entries; Sales-Type Lease; Guaranteed Residual Value) Phelps Company leases a building to Walsh, Inc. on January 1, 2017. The following facts pertain to the lease agreement.

1. The lease term is 5 years, with equal annual rental payments of $4,703 at the beginning of each year.
2. Ownership does not transfer at the end of the lease term, there is no bargain purchase option, and the asset is not of a specialized nature.
3. The building has a fair value of $23,000, a book value to Phelps of $16,000, and a useful life of 6 years.
4. At the end of the lease term, Phelps and Walsh expect there to be an unguaranteed residual value of $4,000.
5. Phelps wants to earn a return of 8% on the lease, and collectibility of the payments is probable. This rate is known by Walsh.

Instructions

(a) How would Phelps (lessor) and Walsh (lessee) classify this lease? How would Phelps initially measure the lease receivable, and how would Walsh initially measure the lease liability and right-of-use asset?

(b) Using the original facts of the lease, show the journal entries to be made by both Phelps and Walsh in 2017.

(c) Suppose the entire expected residual value of $4,000 is guaranteed by Walsh. How will this change your answer to part (a)?

(d) Assume the same facts as part (c), except the expected residual value is $3,000. Does your answer change?

E21-14 (LO 2,4) (Lessee Entries; Initial Direct Costs) Use the information for the Phelps/Walsh lease in E21-13, except that Walsh was unaware of the implicit rate used in the lease by Phelps and has an incremental borrowing rate of 9%.

Instructions

How would your answer to E21-13(a) change?

E21-15 (LO2,4) (Amortization Schedule and Journal Entries for Lessee) Laura Leasing Company signs an agreement on January 1, 2017, to lease equipment to Plote Company. The following information relates to this agreement.

1. The term of the non-cancelable lease is 3 years with no renewal option. The equipment has an estimated economic life of 5 years.
2. The fair value of the asset at January 1, 2017, is $80,000.
3. The asset will revert to the lessor at the end of the lease term, at which time the asset is expected to have a residual value of $7,000, none of which is guaranteed.
4. The agreement requires equal annual rental payments of $25,562.96 to the lessor, beginning on January 1, 2017.
5. The lessee's incremental borrowing rate is 5%. The lessor's implicit rate is 4% and is unknown to the lessee.
6. Plote uses the straight-line depreciation method for all equipment.

Instructions

(Round all numbers to the nearest cent.)

(a) Prepare an amortization schedule that would be suitable for the lessee for the lease term.

(b) Prepare all of the journal entries for the lessee for 2017 and 2018 to record the lease agreement, the lease payments, and all expenses related to this lease. Assume the lessee's annual accounting period ends on December 31.

E21-16 (LO3,4) (Amortization Schedule and Journal Entries for Lessee) Use the information pertaining to Laura Leasing Company and Plote Company from E21-15. Assume that the expected residual value at the end of the lease is $10,000, such that the payments are $24,638.87.

Instructions

Prepare all of the journal entries for the lessee for 2017 to record the lease agreement, the lease payments, and all expenses related to this lease. Assume the lessee's annual accounting period ends on December 31.

E21-17 (LO3,4) (Accounting for an Operating Lease) On January 1, 2017, Nelson Co. leased a building to Wise Inc. The relevant information related to the lease is as follows.

1. The lease arrangement is for 10 years. The building is expected to have a residual value at the end of the lease of $3,500,000 (unguaranteed).
2. The leased building has a cost of $4,000,000 and was purchased for cash on January 1, 2017.
3. The building is depreciated on a straight-line basis. Its estimated economic life is 50 years with no salvage value.
4. Lease payments are $275,000 per year and are made at the beginning of the year.
5. Wise has an incremental borrowing rate of 8%, and the rate implicit in the lease is unknown to Wise.
6. Both the lessor and the lessee are on a calendar-year basis.

Instructions

(a) Prepare the journal entries that Nelson should make in 2017.

(b) Prepare the journal entries that Wise should make in 2017.

(c) If Wise paid $30,000 to a real estate broker on January 1, 2017, as a fee for finding the lessor, how much should Wise report as an expense for this item in 2017?

E21-18 (LO3,4) **(Accounting for an Operating Lease)** On January 1, 2017, a machine was purchased for $900,000 by Young Co. The machine is expected to have an 8-year life with no salvage value. It is to be depreciated on a straight-line basis. The machine was leased to St. Leger Inc. for 3 years on January 1, 2017, with annual rent payments of $150,955 due at the beginning of each year, starting January 1, 2017. The machine is expected to have a residual value at the end of the lease term of $562,500, though this amount is unguaranteed.

Instructions

(a) How much should Young report as income before income tax on this lease for 2017?

(b) Record the journal entries St. Leger would record for 2017 on this lease, assuming its incremental borrowing rate is 6% and the rate implicit in the lease is unknown.

(c) Suppose the lease was only for one year (only one payment of the same amount at commencement of the lease), with a renewal option at market rates at the end of the lease, and St. Leger elects to use the short-term lease exception. Record the journal entries St. Leger would record for 2017 on this lease.

E21-19 (LO3,4) **(Accounting for an Operating Lease)** Kaluzniak Corporation leased equipment to Moeller, Inc. on January 1, 2017. The lease agreement called for annual rental payments of $1,137 at the beginning of each year of the 3-year lease. The equipment has an economic useful life of 7 years, a fair value of $7,000, a book value of $5,000, and Kaluzniak expects a residual value of $4,500 at the end of the lease term. Kaluzniak set the lease payments with the intent of earning a 6% return, though Moeller is unaware of the rate implicit in the lease and has an incremental borrowing rate of 8%. There is no bargain purchase option, ownership of the lease does not transfer at the end of the lease term, and the asset is not of a specialized nature.

Instructions

(a) Describe the nature of the lease to both Kaluzniak and Moeller.

(b) Prepare all necessary journal entries for Moeller in 2017.

(c) How would the measurement of the lease liability and right-of-use asset be affected if, as a result of the lease contract, Moeller was also required to pay $500 in commissions, prepay $750 in addition to the first rental payment, and pay $200 of insurance each year?

(d) Suppose, instead of a 3-year lease term, Moeller and Kaluzniak agree to a one-year lease with a payment of $1,137 at the start of the lease. Prepare all necessary journal entries for Moeller in 2017.

E21-20 (LO3,4) **(Accounting for an Operating Lease)** Use the information for Kaluzniak Corporation and Moeller, Inc. from E21-19.

Instructions

(a) Explain (and show calculations) how Kaluzniak arrived at the amount of the rental payments used in the lease agreement.

(b) Prepare the entries for Kaluzniak for 2017.

(c) How would Kaluzniak's accounting in part (a) change if it incurred legal fees of $700 to execute the lease documents and $500 in advertising expenses for the year in connection with the lease?

E21-21 (LO3,4) **(Accounting for an Operating Lease)** Rauch Incorporated leases a piece of equipment to Donahue Corporation on January 1, 2017. The lease agreement called for annual rental payments of $4,892 at the beginning of each year of the 4-year lease. The equipment has an economic useful life of 6 years, a fair value of $25,000, a book value of $20,000, and both parties expect a residual value of $8,250 at the end of the lease term, though this amount is not guaranteed. Rauch set the lease payments with the intent of earning a 5% return, and Donahue is aware of this rate. There is no bargain purchase option, ownership of the lease does not transfer at the end of the lease term, and the asset is not of a specialized nature.

Instructions

(a) Describe the nature of the lease to both Rauch and Donahue.

(b) Prepare the lease amortization schedule(s) for Donahue for all 4 years of the lease.

(c) Prepare the journal entries for Donahue for 2017 and 2018

(d) Suppose Donahue incurs initial direct costs of $750 related to the lease. Prepare the journal entries for 2017.

(e) Explain how a fully guaranteed residual value by Donahue would change the accounting for the company. The expected residual value is $9,000.

(f) Explain how a bargain renewal option for one extra year at the end of the lease term would change the accounting of the lease for Donahue.

E21-22 (LO3,4) (Accounting for an Operating Lease) Use the information for Rauch Incorporated and Donahue Corporation from E21-21.

Instructions

(a) Explain (and show calculations) how Rauch arrived at the amount of the rental payments used in the lease agreement.

(b) Prepare the entries for Rauch for 2017.

(c) Suppose that instead of $8,250, Rauch expects the residual value at the end of the lease to be $5,000, but Donahue agrees to guarantee a residual value of $8,250. All other facts being equal, how would Rauch change the amount of the annual rental payments, if at all?

(d) Explain how a fully guaranteed residual value by Donahue would change the accounting for Rauch, the lessor.

(e) Explain how a bargain renewal option for one extra year at the end of the lease term would change the accounting of the lease for Rauch, the lessor.

*E21-23 (LO5) (Sale-Leaseback) Assume that on January 1, 2017, Elmer's Restaurants sells a computer system to Liquidity Finance Co. for $680,000 and immediately leases back the computer system. The relevant information is as follows.

1. The computer was carried on Elmer's books at a value of $600,000.

2. The term of the non-cancelable lease is 3 years; title will not transfer to Elmer's, and the expected residual value at the end of the lease is $450,000, all of which is unguaranteed.

3. The lease agreement requires equal rental payments of $115,970 at the beginning of each year.

4. The incremental borrowing rate for Elmer's is 8%. Elmer's is aware that Liquidity Finance set the annual rental to ensure a rate of return of 8%.

5. The computer has a fair value of $680,000 on January 1, 2017, and an estimated economic life of 10 years.

Instructions

Prepare the journal entries for both the lessee and the lessor for 2017 to reflect the sale and leaseback agreement.

*E21-24 (LO5) (Lessee-Lessor, Sale-Leaseback) Respond to the requirements in each situation.

Instructions

(a) On January 1, 2017, Zarle Inc. sold computer equipment to Daniell Co. The sales price of the equipment was $520,000 and its carrying amount is $400,000. Record any journal entries necessary for Zarle from the sale of the computer equipment in 2017.

(b) Use the information from part (a). Assume that, on the same day the sale occurred, Zarle enters into an agreement to lease the equipment from Daniell for 10 years with annual lease payments of $67,342.42 at the end of each year, beginning on December 31, 2017. If Zarle has an incremental borrowing rate of 5% and the equipment has an economic useful life of 10 years, record any journal entries necessary for Zarle from the sale and leaseback of computer equipment in 2017.

(c) Use the information from part (b). Now, instead of 10 years, the lease term is only 3 years with annual lease payments of $67,342.42 at the beginning of each year. Record any journal entries necessary for Zarle from the sale and leaseback of computer equipment in 2017.

*E21-25 (LO6) (Direct Financing Lease) Giannis Corporation leases a building to Jabari, Inc. on January 1, 2017. The following facts pertain to the lease agreement.

1. The lease term is 10 years with equal annual rental payments of $3,449 at the end of each year.

2. Ownership does not transfer at the end of the lease term, there is no bargain purchase option, and the asset is not of a specialized nature.

3. The building has a fair value of $34,000, a book value to Giannis of $22,000, and a useful life of 15 years.

4. At the end of the lease term, Giannis and Jabari expect the residual value of the building to be $12,000, and this amount is guaranteed by Money, Inc., a third party.

5. Giannis wants to earn a 5% return on the lease, and collectibility of the payments is probable.

Instructions

(a) Describe the nature of this lease to both Giannis and Jabari.

(b) Assume the present value of lease payments and third-party guarantee is $34,000 and the rate of return to amortize the net lease receivable to zero is 13.24%. Prepare the amortization schedules Giannis would use to amortize the net lease receivable to zero.

(c) Prepare the journal entries to record the entries for Giannis for 2017 and 2018.

(d) Prepare the journal entries for Jabari (the lessee) for 2017 and 2018, assuming the rate implicit in the lease is known to Jabari.

(e) Suppose the leased asset had a shorter economic life of 8 years, the lease agreement was only for 5 years, and the residual value of $12,000 guaranteed by Money, Inc. remained the same. Would the rate of return required to amortize the net lease receivable to zero increase, decrease, or stay the same? Explain.

(f) Suppose, instead of Money, Inc., Jabari guarantees the residual value itself. How would this affect the classification of this lease agreement for both Giannis and Jabari? Describe the impact that any change in classification would have on revenue recognition for Giannis.

PROBLEMS

P21-1 (LO2,4) (Lessee Entries, Finance Lease) The following facts pertain to a non-cancelable lease agreement between Faldo Leasing Company and Vance Company, a lessee.

Commencement date	January 1, 2017
Annual lease payment due at the beginning of each year, beginning with January 1, 2017	$113,864
Residual value of equipment at end of lease term, guaranteed by the lessee	$50,000
Expected residual value of equipment at end of lease term	$45,000
Lease term	6 years
Economic life of leased equipment	6 years
Fair value of asset at January 1, 2017	$600,000
Lessor's implicit rate	8%
Lessee's incremental borrowing rate	8%

The asset will revert to the lessor at the end of the lease term. The lessee uses the straight-line amortization for all leased equipment.

Instructions

(a) Prepare an amortization schedule that would be suitable for the lessee for the lease term.

(b) Prepare all of the journal entries for the lessee for 2017 and 2018 to record the lease agreement, the lease payments, and all expenses related to this lease. Assume the lessee's annual accounting period ends on December 31.

(c) Suppose Vance received a lease incentive of $5,000 from Faldo Leasing to enter the lease. How would the initial measurement of the lease liability and right-of-use asset be affected? What if Vance prepaid rent of $5,000 to Faldo?

P21-2 (LO2,4) (Lessee Entries and Balance Sheet Presentation, Finance Lease) On January 1, 2017, Cage Company contracts to lease equipment for 5 years, agreeing to make a payment of $120,987 at the beginning of each year, starting January 1, 2017. The leased equipment is to be capitalized at $550,000. The asset is to be amortized on a double-declining-balance basis, and the obligation is to be reduced on an effective-interest basis. Cage's incremental borrowing rate is 6%, and the implicit rate in the lease is 5%, which is known by Cage. Title to the equipment transfers to Cage at the end of the lease. The asset has an estimated useful life of 5 years and no residual value.

Instructions

(a) Explain the probable relationship of the $550,000 amount to the lease arrangement.

(b) Prepare the journal entry or entries that Cage should record on January 1, 2017.

(c) Prepare the journal entries to record amortization of the leased asset and interest expense for the year 2017.

(d) Prepare the journal entry to record the lease payment of January 1, 2018, assuming reversing entries are not made.

(e) What amounts will appear on the lessee's December 31, 2017, balance sheet relative to the lease contract?

(f) How would the value of the lease liability in part (b) change if Cage also agreed to pay the fixed annual insurance on the equipment of $2,000 at the same time as the rental payments?

P21-3 (LO2,4) GROUPWORK (Lessee Entries and Balance Sheet Presentation, Finance Lease) Ludwick Steel Company, as lessee, signed a lease agreement for equipment for 5 years, beginning December 31, 2017. Annual rental payments of $40,000 are to be made at the beginning of each lease year (December 31). The interest rate used by the lessor in setting the payment schedule is 6%; Ludwick's incremental borrowing rate is 8%. Ludwick is unaware of the rate being used by the lessor. At the end of the lease, Ludwick has the option to buy the equipment for $5,000, considerably below its estimated fair value at that time. The equipment has an estimated useful life of 7 years, with no salvage value. Ludwick uses the straight-line method of depreciation on similar owned equipment.

Instructions

(a) Prepare the journal entry or entries, with explanations, that Ludwick should record on December 31, 2017.

(b) Prepare the journal entry or entries, with explanations, that Ludwick should record on December 31, 2018. (Prepare the lease amortization schedule for all five payments.)

(c) Prepare the journal entry or entries, with explanations, that Ludwick should record on December 31, 2019.

(d) What amounts would appear on Ludwick's December 31, 2019, balance sheet relative to the lease arrangement?

P21-4 (LO2) (Lessee Entries, Finance Lease with Monthly Payments) Shapiro Inc. was incorporated in 2016 to operate as a computer software service firm, with an accounting fiscal year ending August 31. Shapiro's primary product is a sophisticated online inventory-control system; its customers pay a fixed fee plus a usage charge for using the system.

Shapiro has leased a large, Alpha-3 computer system from the manufacturer. The lease calls for a monthly rental of $40,000 for the 144 months (12 years) of the lease term. The estimated useful life of the computer is 15 years.

All rentals are payable on the first day of the month beginning with August 1, 2017, the date the computer was installed and the lease agreement was signed. The lease is non-cancelable for its 12-year term, and it is secured only by the manufacturer's chattel lien on the Alpha-3 system.

This lease is to be accounted for as a finance lease by Shapiro, and it will be amortized by the straight-line method. Borrowed funds for this type of transaction would cost Shapiro 6% per year (0.5% per month). Following is a schedule of the present value of an annuity due for selected periods discounted at 0.5% per period when payments are made at the beginning of each period.

Periods (months)	Present Value of an Annuity Due Discounted at 0.5% per Period
1	1.000
2	1.995
3	2.985
143	102.497
144	102.987

Instructions

Prepare all entries Shapiro should make in its accounting records during August 2017 relating to this lease. Give full explanations and show supporting computations for each entry. Remember, August 31, 2017, is the end of Shapiro's fiscal accounting period, and it will be preparing financial statements on that date. Do not prepare closing entries.

P21-5 (LO2,4) (Basic Lessee Accounting with Difficult PV Calculation) In 2016, Grishell Trucking Company negotiated and closed a long-term lease contract for newly constructed truck terminals and freight storage facilities. The buildings were erected to the company's specifications on land owned by the company. On January 1, 2017, Grishell Trucking took possession of the lease properties.

Although the terminals have a composite useful life of 40 years, the non-cancelable lease runs for 20 years from January 1, 2017, with a bargain purchase option available upon expiration of the lease.

The 20-year lease is effective for the period January 1, 2017, through December 31, 2036. Rental payments of $800,000 are payable to the lessor on January 1 of each of the first 10 years of the lease term. Advance rental payments of $320,000 are due on January 1 for each of the last 10 years of the lease. The company has an option to purchase all of these leased facilities for $1 on December 31, 2036. The lease was negotiated to assure the lessor a 6% rate of return.

Instructions

(a) Prepare a schedule to compute for Grishell Trucking the present value of the terminal facilities and related obligation at January 1, 2017.

(b) Assuming that the present value of terminal facilities and related obligation at January 1, 2017, was $7,635,410, prepare journal entries for Grishell Trucking to record the:

(1) Cash payment to the lessor on January 1, 2019.

(2) Amortization of the cost of the leased properties for 2019, using the straight-line method and assuming a zero salvage value.

(3) Accrual of interest expense at December 31, 2019.

Selected present value factors are as follows.

Periods	For an Ordinary Annuity of $1 at 6%	For $1 at 6%
1	.943396	.943396
2	1.833393	.889996
8	6.209794	.627412
9	6.801692	.591898
10	7.360087	.558395
19	11.158117	.330513
20	11.469921	.311805

P21-6 (LO2,4) **(Lessee-Lessor Entries, Finance Lease with a Guaranteed Residual Value)**   Glaus Leasing Company agrees to lease equipment to Jensen Corporation on January 1, 2017. The following information relates to the lease agreement.

1. The term of the lease is 7 years with no renewal option, and the machinery has an estimated economic life of 9 years.
2. The cost of the machinery is $525,000, and the fair value of the asset on January 1, 2017, is $700,000.
3. At the end of the lease term, the asset reverts to the lessor and has a guaranteed residual value of $50,000. Jensen estimates that the expected residual value at the end of the lease term will be $50,000. Jensen amortizes all of its leased equipment on a straight-line basis.
4. The lease agreement requires equal annual rental payments, beginning on January 1, 2017.
5. The collectibility of the lease payments is probable.
6. Glaus desires a 5% rate of return on its investments. Jensen's incremental borrowing rate is 6%, and the lessor's implicit rate is unknown.

Instructions

(Assume the accounting period ends on December 31.)

    (a) Discuss the nature of this lease for both the lessee and the lessor.
    (b) Calculate the amount of the annual rental payment required.
    (c) Compute the value of the lease liability to the lessee.
    (d) Prepare the journal entries Jensen would make in 2017 and 2018 related to the lease arrangement.
    (e) Prepare the journal entries Glaus would make in 2017 and 2018 related to the lease arrangement.
    (f) Suppose Jensen expects the residual value at the end of the lease term to be $40,000 but still guarantees a residual of $50,000. Compute the value of the lease liability at lease commencement.

P21-7 (LO2,4) **(Lessor Computations and Entries, Sales-Type Lease with Guaranteed Residual Value)**   Amirante Inc. manufactures an X-ray machine with an estimated life of 12 years and leases it to Chambers Medical Center for a period of 10 years. The normal selling price of the machine is $495,678, and its guaranteed residual value at the end of the non-cancelable lease term is estimated to be $15,000. The hospital will pay rents of $60,000 at the beginning of each year. Amirante incurred costs of $300,000 in manufacturing the machine and $14,000 in legal fees directly related to the signing of the lease. Amirante has determined that the collectibility of the lease payments is probable and that the implicit interest rate is 5%.

Instructions

    (a) Discuss the nature of this lease in relation to the lessor and compute the amount of each of the following items.
        (1) Lease receivable at commencement of the lease.
        (2) Sales price.
        (3) Cost of sales.
    (b) Prepare a 10-year lease amortization schedule for Amirante, the lessor.
    (c) Prepare all of the lessor's journal entries for the first year.

P21-8 (LO2,4) **(Lessee Computations and Entries, Finance Lease with Guaranteed Residual Value)**   Assume the same data as in P21-7 and that Chambers Medical Center has an incremental borrowing rate of 5% and an expected residual value at the end of the lease of $10,000.

Instructions

    (a) Discuss the nature of this lease in relation to the lessee, and compute the amount of the initial lease liability.
    (b) Prepare a 10-year lease amortization schedule.
    (c) Prepare all of the lessee's journal entries for the first year.
    (d) Suppose Chambers Medical Center incurred $7,000 of document preparation costs after the execution of the lease. How would the initial measurement of the lease liability and right-of-use asset be affected?

P21-9 (L02,4) GROUPWORK (Lessor Computations and Entries, Sales-Type Lease with Unguaranteed Residual Value)
George Company manufactures a check-in kiosk with an estimated economic life of 12 years and leases it to National Airlines for a period of 10 years. The normal selling price of the equipment is $299,140, and its unguaranteed residual value at the end of the lease term is estimated to be $20,000. National will pay annual payments of $40,000 at the beginning of each year. George incurred costs of $180,000 in manufacturing the equipment and $4,000 in sales commissions in closing the lease. George has determined that the collectibility of the lease payments is probable and that the implicit interest rate is 8%.

Instructions

(a) Discuss the nature of this lease in relation to the lessor and compute the amount of each of the following items.

   (1) Lease receivable.

   (2) Sales price.

   (3) Cost of goods sold.

(b) Prepare a 10-year lease amortization schedule for George, the lessor.

(c) Prepare all of the lessor's journal entries for the first year.

P21-10 (L02,4) (Lessee Computations and Entries, Finance Lease with Unguaranteed Residual Value) Assume the same data as in P21-9, with National Airlines having an incremental borrowing rate of 8%.

Instructions

(a) Discuss the nature of this lease in relation to the lessee, and compute the amount of the initial lease liability.

(b) Prepare a 10-year lease amortization schedule.

(c) Prepare all of the lessee's journal entries for the first year. Assume straight-line depreciation.

P21-11 (L02,4) GROUPWORK (Lessee-Lessor Accounting for Residual Values) Goring Dairy leases its milking equipment from King Finance Company under the following lease terms.

1. The lease term is 10 years, non-cancelable, and requires equal rental payments of $30,300 due at the beginning of each year starting January 1, 2017.

2. The equipment has a fair value at the commencement of the lease (January 1, 2017) of $242,741 and a cost of $180,000 on King Finance's books. It also has an estimated economic life of 15 years and an expected residual value of $45,000, though Goring Dairy has guaranteed a residual value of $50,000 to King Finance.

3. The lease contains no renewal options, and the equipment reverts to King Finance upon termination of the lease. The equipment is not of a specialized use.

4. Goring Dairy's incremental borrowing rate is 8% per year. The implicit rate is also 8%.

5. Goring Dairy depreciates similar equipment that it owns on a straight-line basis.

6. Collectibility of the payments is probable.

Instructions

(a) Evaluate the criteria for classification of the lease, and describe the nature of the lease. In general, discuss how the lessee and lessor should account for the lease transaction.

(b) Prepare the journal entries for the lessee and lessor at January 1, 2017, and December 31, 2017 (the lessee's and lessor's year-end). Assume no reversing entries.

(c) What would have been the amount of the initial lease liability recorded by the lessee upon the commencement of the lease if:

   (1) The residual value of $50,000 had been guaranteed by a third party, not the lessee?

   (2) The residual value of $50,000 had not been guaranteed at all?

(d) On the lessor's books, what would be the amount recorded as the lease receivable at the commencement of the lease, assuming:

   (1) The residual value of $50,000 had been guaranteed by a third party?

   (2) The residual value of $50,000 had not been guaranteed at all?

P21-12 (L02,4) (Lessee-Lessor Entries, Balance Sheet Presentation, Finance and Sales-Type Lease) Winston Industries and Ewing Inc. enter into an agreement that requires Ewing Inc. to build three diesel-electric engines to Winston's specifications. Upon completion of the engines, Winston has agreed to lease them for a period of 10 years and to assume all costs and risks of ownership. The lease is non-cancelable, becomes effective on January 1, 2017, and requires annual rental payments of $384,532 each January 1, starting January 1, 2017.

Winston's incremental borrowing rate is 8%. The implicit interest rate used by Ewing and known to Winston is 6%. The total cost of building the three engines is $2,600,000. The economic life of the engines is estimated to be 10 years, with residual value set at zero. Winston depreciates similar equipment on a straight-line basis. At the end of the lease, Winston assumes title to the engines. Collectibility of the lease payments is probable.

Instructions

(a) Discuss the nature of this lease transaction from the viewpoints of both lessee and lessor.

(b) Prepare the journal entry or entries to record the transaction on January 1, 2017, on the books of Winston (the lessee).

(c) Prepare the journal entry or entries to record the transaction on January 1, 2017, on the books of Ewing (the lessor).

(d) Prepare the journal entries for both the lessee and lessor to record the first rental payment on January 1, 2017.

(e) Prepare the journal entries for both the lessee and lessor to record any entries needed in connection with the lease at December 31, 2017. (Prepare a lease amortization schedule for 2 years.)

(f) Show the items and amounts that would be reported on the balance sheet (not notes) at December 31, 2017, for both the lessee and the lessor.

(g) Assume that Winston incurs legal fees related to the execution of the lease of $30,000. In addition, assume Winston receives a lease incentive from Ewing of $50,000 to enter the lease. How will this affect your answer to part (b)?

P21-13 (LO2,4) EXCEL (Balance Sheet and Income Statement Disclosure—Lessee) The following facts pertain to a non-cancelable lease agreement between Alschuler Leasing Company and McKee Electronics, a lessee, for a computer system.

Commencement date	October 1, 2017
Lease term	6 years
Economic life of leased equipment	6 years
Fair value of asset at October 1, 2017	$313,043
Book value of asset at October 1, 2017	$280,000
Residual value at end of lease term	–0–
Lessor's implicit rate	8%
Lessee's incremental borrowing rate	8%
Annual lease payment due at the beginning of each year, beginning with October 1, 2017	$62,700

The collectibility of the lease payments is probable by the lessor. The asset will revert to the lessor at the end of the lease term. The straight-line depreciation method is used for all equipment.

The following amortization schedule has been prepared correctly for use by both the lessor and the lessee in accounting for this lease. The lease is to be accounted for properly as a finance lease by the lessee and as a sales-type lease by the lessor.

Date	Lease Payment/ Receipt	Interest (8%) on Unpaid Liability/Receivable	Reduction of Lease Liability/Receivable	Balance of Lease Liability/Receivable
10/01/17				$313,043
10/01/17	$ 62,700		$ 62,700	250,343
10/01/18	62,700	$20,027	42,673	207,670
10/01/19	62,700	16,614	46,086	161,584
10/01/20	62,700	12,927	49,773	111,811
10/01/21	62,700	8,945	53,755	58,056
10/01/22	62,700	4,644	58,056	–0–
	$376,200	$63,157	$313,043	

Instructions

(a) Assuming the lessee's accounting period ends on September 30, answer the following questions with respect to this lease agreement.

(1) What items and amounts will appear on the lessee's income statement for the year ending September 30, 2018?

(2) What items and amounts will appear on the lessee's balance sheet at September 30, 2018?

(3) What items and amounts will appear on the lessee's income statement for the year ending September 30, 2019?

(4) What items and amounts will appear on the lessee's balance sheet at September 30, 2019?

(b) Assuming the lessee's accounting period ends on December 31, answer the following questions with respect to this lease agreement.

(1) What items and amounts will appear on the lessee's income statement for the year ending December 31, 2017?

(2) What items and amounts will appear on the lessee's balance sheet at December 31, 2017?

(3) What items and amounts will appear on the lessee's income statement for the year ending December 31, 2018?

(4) What items and amounts will appear on the lessee's balance sheet at December 31, 2018?

P21-14 (L02,4) **EXCEL** (Balance Sheet and Income Statement Disclosure—Lessor) Assume the same information as in P21-13.

Instructions

(a) Assuming the lessor's accounting period ends on September 30, answer the following questions with respect to this lease agreement.

   (1) What items and amounts will appear on the lessor's income statement for the year ending September 30, 2018?

   (2) What items and amounts will appear on the lessor's balance sheet at September 30, 2018?

   (3) What items and amounts will appear on the lessor's income statement for the year ending September 30, 2019?

   (4) What items and amounts will appear on the lessor's balance sheet at September 30, 2019?

(b) Assuming the lessor's accounting period ends on December 31, answer the following questions with respect to this lease agreement.

   (1) What items and amounts will appear on the lessor's income statement for the year ending December 31, 2017?

   (2) What items and amounts will appear on the lessor's balance sheet at December 31, 2017?

   (3) What items and amounts will appear on the lessor's income statement for the year ending December 31, 2018?

   (4) What items and amounts will appear on the lessor's balance sheet at December 31, 2018?

P21-15 (L02,3) (Finance and Operating Lease) Anthony Incorporated leases a piece of machinery to Irving Company on January 1, 2017, under the following terms.

1. The lease is to be for 4 years with rental payments of $12,471 to be made at the beginning of each year.
2. The machinery' has a fair value of $67,000, a book value of $50,000, and an economic life of 10 years.
3. At the end of the lease term, both parties expect the machinery to have a residual value of $25,000. To protect against a large loss, Anthony requests Irving to guarantee $17,500 of the residual value, which Irving agrees to do.
4. The lease does not transfer ownership at the end of the lease term, does not have any bargain purchase options, and the asset is not of a specialized nature.
5. The implicit rate is 5%, which is known by Irving.
6. Collectibility of the payments is probable.

Instructions

(a) Evaluate the criteria for classification of the lease, and describe the nature of the lease.

(b) Prepare the journal entries for Irving for the year 2017.

(c) Prepare the journal entries for Anthony for the year 2017.

(d) Suppose Irving did not guarantee any amount of the expected residual value. How would your answers to parts (a)–(c) change?

P21-16 (L03) (Operating Lease) Lewis Corporation entered into a lease agreement on January 1, 2017, to provide Dawkins Company with a piece of machinery. The terms of the lease agreement were as follows.

1. The lease is to be for 3 years with rental payments of $10,521 to be made at the beginning of each year.
2. The machinery has a fair value of $55,000, a book value of $40,000, and an economic life of 8 years.
3. At the end of the lease term, both parties expect the machinery to have a residual value of $30,000, none of which is guaranteed.
4. The lease does not transfer ownership at the end of the lease term, does not have a bargain purchase option, and the asset is not of a specialized nature.
5. The implicit rate is 6%, which is known by Dawkins.
6. Collectibility of the payments is probable.

Instructions

(a) Evaluate the criteria for classification of the lease, and describe the nature of the lease.

(b) Prepare the amortization schedules Dawkins will use over the lease term.

(c) Prepare the 2017 journal entries for Dawkins.

(d) Prepare the 2017 journal entries for Lewis.

(e) Suppose the lease were only for one year instead of 3 years, with just one lease payment at the beginning of the lease term. Prepare any journal entries Dawkins would need, assuming it elects to use the short-term lease option.

P21-17 (L03) **GROUPWORK** (Lessee-Lessor Entries, Operating Lease with an Unguaranteed Residual Value) Cleveland Inc. leased a new crane to Abriendo Construction under a 5-year, non-cancelable contract starting January 1, 2017. Terms of the lease require payments of $48,555 each January 1, starting January 1, 2017. The crane has an estimated life of 7 years, a fair value of $240,000, and a cost to Cleveland of $240,000. The estimated fair value of the crane is expected to be $45,000 (unguaranteed) at the end of the lease term. No bargain purchase or renewal options are included in the contract, and it is not a specialized asset. Both Cleveland and Abriendo adjust and close books annually at December 31. Collectibility of the lease payments is probable. Abriendo's incremental borrowing rate is 8%, and Cleveland's implicit interest rate of 8% is known to Abriendo.

Instructions

(a) Identify the type of lease involved and give reasons for your classification. Discuss the accounting treatment that should be applied by both the lessee and the lessor.

(b) Prepare all the entries related to the lease contract and leased asset for the year 2017 for the lessee and lessor, assuming Abriendo uses straight-line amortization for all similar leased assets, and Cleveland depreciates the asset on a straight-line basis with a salvage value of $15,000.

(c) Discuss what should be presented in the balance sheet, the income statement, and the related notes of both the lessee and the lessor at December 31, 2017.

CONCEPTS FOR ANALYSIS

CA21-1 WRITING (Lessee Accounting and Reporting) On January 1, 2017, Evans Company entered into a non-cancelable lease for a machine to be used in its manufacturing operations. The lease transfers control of the machine to Evans by the end of the lease term. The term of the lease is 8 years, which equals the useful life of the asset. The lease payment made by Evans on January 1, 2017, was one of eight equal annual payments. At the commencement of the lease, the criteria established for classification as a finance lease by the lessee were met.

Instructions

(a) What is the theoretical basis for the accounting standard that requires certain long-term leases to be capitalized by the lessee? Do not discuss the specific criteria for classifying a specific lease as a finance lease.

(b) How should Evans account for this lease at its commencement?

(c) What expenses directly related to lease liability and right-of-use asset will Evans incur during the first year of the lease, and how will these expenses be determined?

(d) How should Evans report the lease transaction on its December 31, 2017, balance sheet?

CA21-2 (Lessor and Lessee Accounting and Disclosure) Sylvan Inc. entered into a non-cancelable lease arrangement with Breton Leasing Corporation for a certain machine. Breton's primary business is leasing. Sylvan will lease the machine for a period of 3 years, which is 50% of the machine's economic life. Breton will take possession of the machine at the end of the initial 3-year lease and lease it to another, smaller company that does not need the most current version of the machine. Sylvan does not guarantee any residual value for the machine and will not purchase the machine at the end of the lease term. Sylvan's incremental borrowing rate is 10%, and the implicit rate in the lease is 9%. Sylvan has no way of knowing the implicit rate used by Breton. Using either rate, the present value of the lease payments is between 90% and 100% of the fair value of the machine at the date of the lease agreement. Breton is reasonably certain that Sylvan will pay all lease payments.

Instructions

(a) With respect to Sylvan (the lessee), answer the following.
  (1) What type of lease has been entered into? Explain the reason for your answer.
  (2) How should Sylvan compute the appropriate amount to be recorded for the lease or asset acquired?
  (3) What accounts will be created or affected by this transaction, and how will the lease or asset and other costs related to the transaction be recorded in earnings?
  (4) What disclosures must Sylvan make regarding this leased asset?

(b) With respect to Breton (the lessor), answer the following.
  (1) What type of leasing arrangement has been entered into? Explain the reason for your answer.
  (2) How should this lease be recorded by Breton, and how are the appropriate amounts determined?
  (3) How should Breton determine the appropriate amount of revenue to be recognized from each lease payment?
  (4) What disclosures must Breton make regarding this lease?

CA21-3 (Lessee Capitalization Tests) On January 1, Santiago Company, a lessee, entered into three non-cancelable leases for new equipment, Lease L, Lease M, and Lease N. None of the three leases transfers ownership of the equipment to Santiago at the end of the lease term. For each of the three leases, the present value at the beginning of the lease term of the lease payments is 75% of the fair value of the equipment. The following information is specific to each lease.

1. Lease L does not contain a bargain purchase option. The lease term is equal to 80% of the estimated economic life of the equipment.
2. Lease M contains a bargain purchase option. The lease term is equal to 50% of the estimated economic life of the equipment.
3. Lease N does not contain a bargain purchase option. The lease term is equal to 50% of the estimated economic life of the equipment.

Instructions

(a) How should Santiago classify each of the three leases above, and why? Discuss the rationale for your answer.

(b) What amount, if any, should Santiago record as a liability at commencement of the lease for each of the three leases above?

(c) Assuming that the lease payments are made on a straight-line basis, how should Santiago record each lease payment for each of the three leases above?

CA21-4 (Comparison of Different Types of Accounting by Lessee and Lessor)

Part 1: Finance leases and operating leases are the two classifications of leases described in FASB pronouncements from the standpoint of the **lessee.**

Instructions

(a) Describe how a finance lease would be accounted for by the lessee both at the commencement of the lease and during the first year of the lease, assuming the lease transfers ownership of the property to the lessee by the end of the lease.

(b) Describe how an operating lease would be accounted for by the lessee both at the commencement of the lease and during the first year of the lease, assuming equal monthly payments are made by the lessee at the beginning of each month of the lease.

Do **not** discuss the criteria for distinguishing between finance leases and operating leases.

Part 2: Sales-type leases and operating leases are two of the classifications of leases described in FASB pronouncements from the standpoint of the **lessor.**

Instructions

Compare and contrast a sales-type lease with an operating lease as follows.

(a) Lease receivable.

(b) Recognition of interest revenue.

(c) Gross profit.

Do **not** discuss the criteria for distinguishing between the leases described above and operating leases.

CA21-5 ETHICS (Lease Capitalization, Bargain Purchase Option) Baden Corporation entered into a lease agreement for 100 photocopy machines for its corporate headquarters. The lease agreement qualifies as an operating lease except there is a bargain purchase option. After the 5-year lease term, the corporation can purchase each copier for $1,000, when the anticipated fair value is $2,500.

Jerry Suffolk, the financial vice president, thinks the financial statements must recognize the lease agreement as a finance lease because of the bargain purchase option. The controller, Diane Buchanan, disagrees: "Although I don't know much about the copiers themselves, there is a way to avoid recording the lease liability." She argues that the corporation might claim that copier technology advances rapidly and that by the end of the lease term, the machines will most likely not be worth the $1,000 bargain price.

Instructions

(a) What ethical issue is at stake?

(b) Should the controller's argument be accepted if she does not really know much about copier technology? Would it make a difference if the controller were knowledgeable about the rate of change in copier technology?

(c) What should Suffolk do?

CA21-6 WRITING (Short-Term Lease vs. Finance Lease) You are auditing the December 31, 2017, financial statements of Hockney, Inc., manufacturer of novelties and party favors. During your inspection of the company garage, you discovered that a used automobile not listed in the equipment subsidiary ledger is parked there. You ask Stacy Reeder, plant manager, about the vehicle, and she tells you that the company did not list the automobile because the company was only leasing it and elected to use the short-term lease accounting option for the lease. The lease agreement was entered into on January 1, 2017, with Crown New and Used Cars.

You decide to review the lease agreement to ensure that the lease should be afforded short-term lease treatment, and you discover the following lease terms.

1. Non-cancelable term of 2 years.
2. Rental of $3,240 per year (at the end of each year). (The present value at 8% per year is $5,778.)
3. Expected residual value after 2 years is $500. (The present value at 8% per year is $429.) Hockney guarantees the residual value of $500.
4. Estimated economic life of the automobile is 2.5 years.
5. Hockney's incremental borrowing rate is 8% per year.

Instructions

You are a senior auditor writing a memo to your supervisor, the audit partner in charge of this audit, to discuss the above situation. Be sure to include (a) why you inspected the lease agreement, (b) what you determined about the lease, and (c) how you advised your client to account for this lease. Explain every journal entry that you believe is necessary to record this lease properly on the client's books. (It is also necessary to include the fact that you communicated this information to your client.)

***CA21-7** (Sale-Leaseback)** On January 1, 2017, Perriman Company transferred equipment for cash and leased it back. As seller-lessee, Perriman retained the right to substantially all of the remaining use of the equipment. The term of the lease is 8 years.

Instructions

   (a) What is the major issue related to sale-leaseback accounting?
   (b) **(1)** How should Perriman account for the sale portion of the sale-leaseback transaction at January 1, 2017?
        (2) How should Perriman account for the leaseback portion of the sale-leaseback transaction at January 1, 2017?

USING YOUR JUDGMENT

Note that P&G, Delta Air Lines, Southwest Airlines, and Wal-Mart have not yet adopted the new lease accounting rules. As a result, in the financial statements referred to below, finance leases are referred to as "capital," and assets and liabilities related to operating leases are not recognized on the balance sheet.

Financial Reporting Problem

The Procter & Gamble Company (P&G)

The financial statements of P&G are presented in Appendix B. The company's complete annual report, including the notes to the financial statements, is available online.

Instructions

Refer to P&G's financial statements, accompanying notes, and management's discussion and analysis to answer the following questions.

   (a) What types of leases are used by P&G?
   (b) What amount of capital leases was reported by P&G in total and for less than one year?
   (c) What minimum annual rental commitments under all non-cancelable leases at June 30, 2014, did P&G disclose?

Comparative Analysis Case

Delta Air Lines and Southwest Airlines

The financial statements and notes to the financial statements for Delta Air Lines and Southwest Airlines can be found online.

Instructions

Use information found in the companies' financial reports to answer the following questions.

   (a) What types of leases are used by Southwest and on what assets are these leases primarily used?
   (b) How long-term are some of Southwest's leases? What are some of the characteristics or provisions of Southwest's (as lessee) leases?
   (c) What did Southwest report in 2014 as its future minimum annual rental commitments under non-cancelable leases?
   (d) At year-end 2014, what was the present value of the minimum rental payments under Southwest's capital leases? How much imputed interest was deducted from the future minimum annual rental commitments to arrive at the present value?
   (e) What were the amounts and details reported by Southwest for rental expense in 2014, 2013, and 2012?
   (f) How does Delta's use of leases compare with Southwest's?

Financial Statement Analysis Case

Wal-Mart Stores, Inc.

The following are the financial statement disclosures from the January 31, 2015, annual report of Wal-Mart Stores, Inc.

Wal-Mart Stores, Inc.
(dollar amounts in millions)

	Jan. 31, 2015	Jan. 31, 2014	
Current Liabilities			Description and amount of lease obligations
Obligations under capital leases due within one year	$ 287	$ 309	
Noncurrent Liabilities			
Long-term obligations under capital leases	$2,606	$2,788	

Note 12: Commitments

The Company has long-term leases for stores and equipment. Rentals (including amounts applicable to taxes, insurance, maintenance, other operating expenses and contingent rentals) under operating leases and other short-term rental arrangements were $2.8 billion in both fiscal 2015 and 2014. Aggregate minimum annual rental at January 31, 2015, under non-cancelable leases are as follows (dollar amounts in millions):

General description and amount of lease rental expense

	Operating Leases	Capital Leases	
2016	$1,759	$ 504	
2017	1,615	476	Description and amounts of leased assets
2018	1,482	444	
2019	1,354	408	
2020	1,236	370	
Thereafter	10,464	3,252	
Total minimum rentals	17,910	$5,454	
Less estimated executor costs		49	
Net minimum lease payments		$5,405	
Less imputed interest		2,512	
Present value of minimum lease payments		$2,893	Nature, timing, and amounts of cash outflows

Certain of the Company's leases provide for the payment of contingent rentals based on a percentage of sales. Such contingent rentals were immaterial for fiscal 2015 and 2014. Substantially all of the Company's store leases have renewal options, some of winch may trigger an escalation in rentals. The Company has future lease commitments for land and buildings for approximately 282 future locations. These lease commitments have lease terms ranging from 1 to 30 years and provide for certain minimum rentals. If executed, payments under operating leases would increase by $58 million for fiscal 2016, based on current cost estimates.

Instructions

Answer the following questions related to these disclosures.

(a) What is the total obligation under capital leases at January 31, 2015, for Wal-Mart?

(b) What is the total rental expense reported for leasing activity for the year ended January 31, 2015, for Wal-Mart?

(c) Estimate the off-balance-sheet liability due to Wal-Mart's operating leases at January 31, 2015.

Accounting, Analysis, and Principles

Salaur Company, a risky start-up, is evaluating a lease arrangement being offered by TSP Company for use of a standard computer system. The lease is non-cancelable, and in no case does Salaur receive title to the computers during or at the end of the lease term. TSP will lease the returned computers to other customers. The lease starts on January 1, 2017, with the first rental payment due on January 1, 2017. Additional information related to the lease and the underlying leased asset is as follows.

Yearly rental	$3,057.25
Lease term	3 years
Estimated economic life	5 years
Purchase option	$3,000 at end of 3 years, which approximates fair value
Renewal option	1 year at $1,500; no penalty for nonrenewal; standard renewal clause
Fair value at commencement	$10,000
Cost of asset to lessor	$8,000
Residual value:	
Guaranteed	–0–
Unguaranteed	$3,000
Lessor's implicit rate (known by the lessee)	12%
Estimated fair value at end of lease	$3,000

Accounting

(a) Analyze the lease classification tests for this lease for Salaur. Prepare the journal entries for Salaur for 2017.

(b) Repeat the requirements in part (a), assuming Salaur has the option to purchase the system at the end of the lease for $100.

Analysis

Briefly discuss the impact of the accounting for this lease as a finance or operating lease for two common ratios: return on assets and debt to total assets.

Principles

What fundamental quality of useful information is being addressed when a company like Salaur capitalizes all leases with terms of one year or longer?

BRIDGE TO THE PROFESSION

FASB Codification References

[1] FASB ASC 842 (Glossary). [Predecessor literature: None.]

[2] FASB ASC 842-10-25-2. [Predecessor literature: None.]

[3] FASB ASU 2016-2 [BC 71(c).] [Predecessor literature: None.]

[4] FASB ASU 2016-2 (BC 194, 197, 218). [Predecessor literature: None.]

[5] FASB ASC 842 (Glossary). [Predecessor literature: None.]

[6] FASB ASC 842-20-30-3. [Predecessor literature: None.]

[7] FASB ASC 842 (Glossary). [Predecessor literature: None.]

[8] FASB ASC 842-10-30-5(f). [Predecessor literature: None.]

[9] FASB ASC 842-20-40-2. [Predecessor literature: None.]

[10] FASB ASU 2016-2 (BC 93). [Predecessor literature: None.]

[11] FASB ASC 842-10-25-3(a). [Predecessor literature: None.]

[12] FASB ASC 842-30-25-3(b). [Predecessor literature: None.]

[13] FASB ASU 2016-2 (BC 61). [Predecessor literature: None.]

[14] FASB ASC 842-10-55-34 to 36. [Predecessor literature: None.]

[15] FASB ASC 842-10-15-30. [Predecessor literature: None.]

[16] FASB ASC 842 (Glossary). [Predecessor literature: None.]

[17] FASB ASC 842-30-25-1(c), 8, 10. [Predecessor literature: None.]

[18] FASB ASC 842-20-25-2. [Predecessor literature: None.]

[19] FASB ASC 842-20-50 and 842-30-50. [Predecessor literature: None.]

[20] FASB ASC 842-40-25, 842-40-30, and 842-40-50. [Predecessor literature: None.]

[21] FASB ASC 842-10-25-3; ASU 2016-2 (BC95-96). [Predecessor literature: None.]

[22] FASB ASC 842-30-25-9. [Predecessor literature: None.]

[23] FASB ASC 842-30-25-8. [Predecessor literature: None.]

Codification Exercises

If your school has a subscription to the FASB Codification, go to *http://aaahq.org/ascLogin.cfm* to log in and prepare responses to the following. Provide Codification references for your responses.

CE21-1 Access the glossary ("Master Glossary") to answer the following.
- **(a)** What is the "commencement date"?
- **(b)** What is the definition of "incremental borrowing rate"?
- **(c)** What is an unguaranteed residual asset?
- **(d)** What are variable lease payments?

CE21-2 What comprises lease payments? What is excluded?

CE21-3 What information should a lessee disclose about its finance leases in its financial statements and footnotes?

CE21-4 How should a lessor measure its net investment in either a sales-type lease or a direct financing lease?

Codification Research Case

Daniel Hardware Co. is considering alternative financing arrangements for equipment used in its warehouses. Besides purchasing the equipment outright, Daniel is also considering a lease. Accounting for the outright purchase is fairly straightforward, but because Daniel has not used equipment leases in the past, the accounting staff is less informed about the specific accounting rules for leases. The staff is aware of some general lease rules related to "right-of-use," but they are unsure how the accounting rules apply to their situation. Daniel has asked you to conduct some research on these items related to lease capitalization criteria.

Instructions

If your school has a subscription to the FASB Codification, go to *http://aaahq.org/ascLogin.cfm* to log in and prepare responses to the following. Provide Codification references for your responses.

- **(a)** What is included is the measurement of (1) the lease liability and (2) the right-of-use asset?
- **(b)** Besides the non-cancelable term of the lease, what other considerations determine the "lease term"?
- **(c)** When should a lessee account for a lease modification? What procedures are followed?

ADDITIONAL PROFESSIONAL RESOURCES

Go to **WileyPLUS** for other career-readiness resources, such as career coaching, internship opportunities, and CPAexcel prep.

IFRS Insights

LEARNING OBJECTIVE 8	Leasing is a global business. Lessors and lessees enter into arrangements with one another without regard to national boundaries. Although GAAP and IFRS for leasing are not identical, both the FASB and the IASB decided that prior lease accounting did not provide the most useful, transparent, and complete information about leasing transactions. In response, the FASB and IASB worked together on a lease accounting project. The IASB issued *IFRS 16, Leases* in January 2016. Many of the requirements in the new FASB standard are the same as those in *IFRS 16*. The main differences between GAAP and IFRS under the new rules are in relation to the lessee accounting model. Specifically, IFRS does not make a distinction between finance leases and operating leases in the financial statements. As a result, lessees account for all leases using the finance lease method.
Compare the accounting for leases under GAAP and IFRS.	

RELEVANT FACTS

Following are the key similarities and differences between GAAP and IFRS related to the accounting for leases.

Similarities

- Both GAAP and IFRS share the same objective of recording leases by lessees and lessors according to their economic substance—that is, according to the definitions of assets and liabilities.
- Much of the terminology for lease accounting in IFRS and GAAP is the same.

- Both GAAP and IFRS require lessees to recognize a right-of-use asset and related lease liability for leases with terms longer than one year.
- Under both IFRS and GAAP, lessors use the same general criteria (consistent with the recent standard on revenue) to determine if there is transfer of control of the underlying asset and if lessors classify leases as sales-type or operating.
- GAAP and IFRS use the same lessor accounting model for leases classified as sales-type or operating.
- GAAP and IFRS have similar qualitative and quantitative disclosure requirements for lessees and lessors.

Differences

- There is no classification test for lessees under *IFRS 16*. Thus, lessees account for all leases using the finance lease method—that is, leases classified as operating leases under GAAP will be accounted for differently compared to IFRS (see example in About the Numbers section below).
- IFRS allows alternative measurement bases for the right-of-use asset (e.g., the revaluation model, in accordance with *IAS 16, Property, Plant and Equipment*).
- In addition to the short-term lease exception, IFRS has an additional lessee recognition and measurement exemption for leases of assets of low value (e.g., personal computers, small office furniture).
- IFRS does not include any explicit guidance on collectibility of the lease payments by lessors and amounts necessary to satisfy a residual value guarantee.
- IFRS does not distinguish between sales-type and direct financing leases for lessors. Therefore, *IFRS 16* permits recognition of selling profit on direct financing leases at lease commencement.

ABOUT THE NUMBERS

A **lease** is defined as "a contract, or part of a contract, that conveys the right to control the use of an identified property, plant or equipment (an identified asset) for a period of time in exchange for consideration." A lease therefore conveys use of an asset from one party (the lessor) to another (the lessee) without transferring ownership. Accounting for lease transactions is controversial as the following example illustrates.

If Air France borrows $47 million on a 10-year note from Bank of America to purchase a Boeing 737 jet plane, Air France should report an asset and related liability at that amount on its statement of financial position. Similarly, if Air France purchases the 737 for $47 million directly from Boeing through an installment purchase over 10 years, it should report an asset and related liability (i.e., it should "capitalize" the installment transaction).

However, what if Air France **leases** the Boeing 737 for 10 years from International Lease Finance Corp. (ILFC)—the world's largest lessor of airplanes—through a non-cancelable lease transaction with payments of the same amount as the installment purchase transaction? In that case, opinion differs over how to report this transaction. Views on the appropriate accounting range from no capitalization to capitalization of all long-term leases.

The IASB now requires companies to capitalize all leases. The only exceptions to this guideline is that leases covering a term of less than one year or leases under $5,000 do not have to be capitalized. The IASB indicates that the right to use property under the terms of the lease is an asset, and the lessee's obligation to make payments under the lease is a liability. As a result, Air France records the right-of-use of the airplane as an asset on its statement of financial position. It also records a liability for its obligation to make payments under the lease.

Lessee Accounting

Lessees use the finance lease method to account for all non-cancelable leases, by recording a right-of-use asset and related lease liability. The lessee recognizes interest expense on the lease liability over the life of the lease using the effective-interest method and records depreciation expense on the right-of-use asset. This accounting is applied whether the lease arrangement is effectively a purchase of the underlying asset (Air France's lease with ILFC above) or the lessee **obtains control of only the use of the underlying asset**, but not the underlying asset itself. For example, a lease may convey use of one floor of an office building for five years. At the end of the lease, the lessee vacates the floor and the lessor can then lease the floor to another tenant. In this situation, the lease conveys right-of-use but not ownership. However, lessee accounting for leases that transfer ownership or transfer control is the same.

Lessee Accounting at Commencement

At commencement of the lease, lessees record a right-of-use asset and lease liability. The measurement of the right-of-use asset depends on the lease liability. The lease liability is computed as the present value of the lease payments. An asset for the right-of-use of the underlying asset (i.e., the right-of-use asset) is equal to the lease liability, adjusted for prepaid rent (less lease incentives received from the lessor), and any initial direct costs.[27]

Subsequent Lessee Accounting

Throughout the term of the lease, a lessee, like Air France, uses the **effective-interest method** to allocate each lease payment between principal and interest on the lease liability. This method produces a periodic interest expense equal to a constant percentage of the carrying value of the lease obligation. When applying the effective-interest method to finance leases, Air France must use the same discount rate (the implicit rate) that determines the present value of the lease payments.

Depreciation of the right-of-use asset is accounted for similar to other non-financial assets. That is, the lessee should depreciate the right-of-use asset using an approach that reflects the consumption of the economic benefits of the leased asset. Generally, companies use the straight-line method for recording the consumption of a right-of-use asset. One troublesome aspect of accounting for the depreciation of the right-of-use asset relates to the depreciable life. If the lease agreement transfers ownership of the asset to Air France or if the lease contains a bargain purchase option at the end of the lease, Air France depreciates the aircraft consistent with its normal depreciation policy for other aircraft, **using the economic life of the asset**. On the other hand, if the lease does not transfer ownership and does not contain a bargain purchase option at the end of the lease, then Air France depreciates it over the **term of the lease**. In this case, the aircraft reverts to ILFC after a certain period of time.

Recognizing the interest on the lease liability coupled with the depreciation of the right-of-use asset will **generally result in higher total expense in the earlier years and lower total expense in the later years of the lease**.

Lease Accounting Example

To illustrate lessee accounting for a lease that conveys right-of-use but not ownership, assume that Hathaway Disposal Inc. (lessor) and Marks and Spencer plc (M&S) (the lessee) sign a lease agreement dated January 1, 2017. The lease agreement specifies that Hathaway will grant right-of-use of one of its standard cardboard compactors for use at one of M&S's stores. Information relevant to the lease is as follows.

- The term of the lease is three years. The lease agreement is non-cancelable, requiring equal rental payments of $17,620.08 at the beginning of each year of the lease (annuity-due basis).
- The compactor has a cost and fair value at commencement of the lease of $60,000, an estimated economic life of seven years, and a residual value of $12,000 (unguaranteed).
- The lease contains no renewal options, and the compactor reverts to Hathaway at the termination of the lease.
- The implicit rate of the lessor is not known by M&S. M&S's incremental borrowing rate is 6 percent.

Under this lease arrangement, M&S has right of use of the compactor for three years and will return the asset to Hathaway at the end of the lease; Hathaway retains ownership of the compactor. Illustration IFRS21-1 shows the present value of the lease payments for M&S in this situation is $49,924.56 ($17,620.08 × 2.83339). M&S makes the following entries to record the lease and the first payment.

January 1, 2017

Right-of-Use Asset	49,924.56	
Lease Liability		49,924.56
(To record the right-of-use asset and related liability at commencement of the lease)		
Lease Liability	17,620.08	
Cash		17,620.08
(To record first lease payment)		

M&S prepares a lease amortization schedule to show interest expense and related amortization of the lease liability over the three-year period, as shown in Illustration IFRS21-1.

---

[27]Determination of elements of the lease liability (lease payment, discounts. rate) and the right-of-use asset is the same under IFRS and GAAP.

MARKS AND SPENCER PLC
LEASE AMORTIZATION SCHEDULE
ANNUITY-DUE BASIS

Date	Lease Payment (a)	Interest (6%) on Liability (b)	Reduction of Lease Liability (c)	Lease Liability (d)
1/1/17				$49,924.56
1/1/17	$17,620.08	$ –0–	$17,620.08	32,304.48
1/1/18	17,620.08	1,938.27	15,681.81	16,622.67
1/1/19	17,620.08	997.41*	16,622.67	0.00
	$52,860.24	$2,935.68	$49,924.56	

(a) Lease payment as required by lease.
(b) Six percent of the preceding balance of (d) except for 1/1/17; since this is an annuity due, no time has elapsed at the date of the first payment and therefore no interest has accrued.
(c) (a) minus (b).
(d) Preceding balance minus (c).

*Rounded by $0.05.

The journal entries to be prepared by M&S throughout the lease to record lease expense and amortization of the lease liability and depreciation of the right-of-use asset are as follows, using the amounts presented in Illustration IFRS21-2.

Marks and Spencer plc (Lessee)

Recognize lease expense, record amortization (December 31, 2017):		
Interest Expense	1,938.27	
Lease Liability		1,938.27
Depreciation Expense	16,641.52	
Accumulated Depreciation (Right-of-Use Asset)		
($49,924.56 ÷ 3)		16,641.52
Record second lease payment (January 1, 2018):		
Lease Liability ($1,938.27 + $15,681.81)	17,620.08	
Cash		17,620.08
Recognize lease expense, record amortization (December 31, 2018):		
Interest Expense	997.41	
Lease Liability		997.41
Depreciation Expense	16,641.52	
Accumulated Depreciation (Right-of-Use Asset)		
($49,924.56 ÷ 3)		16,641.52
Record third lease payment (January 1, 2019):		
Lease Liability ($997.41 + $16,622.67)	17,620.08	
Cash		17,620.08
Record amortization (December 31, 2019):		
Depreciation Expense	16,641.52	
Accumulated Depreciation (Right-of-Use Asset)		
($49,924.56 ÷ 3)		16,641.52

Following these entries, as indicated in Illustration IFRS21-1, the lease liability and the right-of-use asset have zero balances.[28] M&S returns the asset to Hathaway.

[28]Under GAAP, this lease is classified as an operating lease and lease expense is be recognized on a straight-line basis. Lessor accounting for an operating lease under IFRS and GAAP is essentially the same; that is, the lessor records Lease Revenue in each year of the lease on a straight-line basis.

ON THE HORIZON

Lease accounting is one of the areas identified in the IASB/FASB Memorandum of Understanding. The Boards have developed rules based on "right-of-use" (ROU) which require that all leases with terms longer than one year be recorded on the statement of financial position/balance sheet. The IASB has decided on a single approach for lessee accounting. Under the IASB approach, a lessee accounts for all leases as finance leases, recognizing depreciation of the ROU asset separately from interest on the lease liability. The FASB reached a different conclusion on the expense recognition for operating-type leases. Under the FASB model, the income effects will reflect a straight-line expense pattern, reported as a single total lease expense. The Boards are generally converged with respect to lessor accounting.

IFRS SELF-TEST QUESTIONS

1. Which of the following is **not** true with respect to lease accounting under IFRS?

   (a) IFRS require lessees to recognize a right-of-use asset and related lease liability for leases with terms longer than one year.
   (b) IFRS does not include any explicit guidance on collectibility of the lease payments by lessors and amounts necessary to satisfy a residual value guarantee.
   (c) IFRS does not permit recognition of selling profit on direct financing leases at lease commencement.
   (d) IFRS uses essentially the same lessor accounting model as GAAP for leases classified as sales-type or operating.

2. Under IFRS:

   (a) lessees and lessors recognize right-of-use assets.
   (b) lessees always use the operating method.
   (c) lessees always recognize a right-of-use asset and lease liability for leases with terms less than one year.
   (d) lessors do not distinguish between sales-type and direct financing leases.

3. All of the following are similarities with respect to the accounting for leases, under IFRS and GAAP, **except**:

   (a) lessees recognize a right-of-use asset and related lease liability for leases with terms longer than one year.
   (b) lessees use the same general lease classification criteria to determine if lessees classify leases as finance or operating.

   (c) lessors under IFRS and GAAP use the same model to account for sales-type leases.
   (d) GAAP and IFRS have similar qualitative and quantitative disclosure requirements for lessees and lessors.

4. Under IFRS:

   (a) lessees may use alternative measurement bases (e.g., revaluation accounting) for the right-of-use asset.
   (b) different measurement bases may be used for the right-of-use asset but only for leases with terms less than one year.
   (c) the same guidance on collectibility of the lease payments is used by lessors as in GAAP.
   (d) lessors are required to defer gross profit on direct financing leases.

5. All of the following are differences with respect to the accounting for leases, under IFRS and GAAP, **except**:

   (a) IFRS has an additional lessee recognition and measurement exemption for leases of assets of low value (GAAP does not).
   (b) IFRS allows alternative measurement bases for the right-of-use asset (e.g., the revaluation model).
   (c) under IFRS, lessees use the same tests to determine if a lease should be classified as finance or operating.
   (d) IFRS permits recognition of selling profit on direct financing leases at lease commencement.

IFRS CONCEPTS AND APPLICATION

IFRS21-1 Where can authoritative IFRS related to the accounting for leases be found?

IFRS21-2 Briefly describe some of the similarities and differences between GAAP and IFRS with respect to the accounting for leases.

IFRS21-3 Outline the accounting procedures (the finance lease method) for a lease by a lessee.

IFRS21-4 Kleckner Corporation recorded a lease at $300,000 on December 31, 2016. Kleckner's incremental borrowing rate is 8%, and the implicit rate of the lessor is not known. Kleckner made the first lease payment of $48,337 on December 31, 2016. The lease requires eight annual payments. The equipment has a useful life of 8 years with no residual value. Prepare Kleckner's December 31, 2017, adjusting entries.

IFRS21-5 Use the information for Kleckner Corporation from IFRS21-4. Assume that at December 31, 2017, Kleckner made an adjusting entry to accrue interest expense of $20,133 on the lease. Prepare Kleckner's January 1, 2018, journal entry to record the second lease payment of $48,337.

IFRS21-6 Delaney Company leases an automobile with a fair value of $10,000 from Simon Motors, Inc., on the following terms.

1. Non-cancelable term of 50 months.
2. Rental of $200 per month at the beginning of each month. (The present value at 0.5% per month is $8,873.)
3. Estimated economic life of the automobile is 60 months.
4. Delaney's incremental borrowing rate is 6% a year (0.5% a month). Simon's implicit rate is unknown.

Instructions

(a) What is the present value of the lease payments to determine the lease liability?
(b) Record the lease on Delaney's books at the commencement date.
(c) Record the first month's lease payment (at commencement of the lease).
(d) Record the second month's lease payment.
(e) Record the first month's depreciation on Delaney's books (assume straight-line).

IFRS21-7 On January 1, 2017, a machine was purchased for $900,000 by Young Co. The machine is expected to have an 8-year life with no residual value. It is to be depreciated on a straight-line basis. The machine was leased to St. Ledger Inc. for 3 years on January 1, 2017, with annual rent payments of $150,955 due each December 31, though St. Ledger was required to prepay the last year's rent on the commencement date. The machine is expected to have a residual value at the end of the lease term of $562,500, though this amount is unguaranteed.

Instructions

(a) Record the journal entries St. Ledger would record for 2017 on this lease, assuming its incremental borrowing rate is 6% and the implicit rate is unknown.
(b) Suppose the lease was only for one year (only one payment of the same amount at the commencement of the lease), with a renewal option at market rates at the end of the lease, and St. Ledger elects to use the short-term lease exception. Record the journal entries St. Ledger would record for 2017 on this lease.
(c) How much should Young report as income before income tax on this operating lease for 2017?

Professional Research

IFRS21-8 Daniel Hardware Co. is considering alternative financing arrangements for equipment used in its warehouses. Besides purchasing the equipment outright, Daniel is also considering a lease. Accounting for the outright purchase is fairly straightforward, but because Daniel has not used equipment leases in the past, the accounting staff is less informed about the specific accounting rules for leases. The staff is aware of some general lease rules related to "right-of-use," but they are unsure how the accounting rules apply to their situation. Daniel has asked you to conduct some research on these items related to lease capitalization criteria.

Instructions

Access the IFRS authoritative literature at the IASB website (*http://eifrs.iasb.org/*). (Click on the IFRS tab and then register for free eIFRS access if necessary.) When you have accessed the documents, you can use the search tool in your Internet browser to respond to the following questions. (Provide paragraph citations.)

(a) What is included is the measurement of (1) the lease liability and (2) the right-of-use asset?
(b) Besides the non-cancelable term of the lease, what are other considerations in determining the "lease term?"
(c) When should a lessee account for a lease modification? What procedures are followed?

International Financial Reporting Problem

Marks and Spencer plc (M&S)

IFRS21-9 The financial statements of M&S are presented in Appendix E. The company's complete annual report, including the notes to the financial statements, is available online.

Instructions
Refer to M&S's financial statements and the accompanying notes to answer the following questions.

(a) What types of leases are used by M&S?

(b) What amount of finance leases was reported by M&S in total and for less than one year?

(c) What minimum annual rental commitments under all non-cancelable leases at 28 March 2015 did M&S disclose?

ANSWERS TO IFRS SELF-TEST QUESTIONS

1. c **2.** d **3.** b **4.** a **5.** c

Printed in the USA
K075498SCI122917   01S29053000000002729